SHAMANIC WISDOM II:
The Way of the Animal Spirits

DOLFYN & SWIMMING WOLF

ISBN # 0-929268-18-0

Diane Versteeg

is an artist whose love for animals is beautifully expressed by the drawings in this book. She specializes exclusively in animal art, and is available for commissions on a freelance basis. Limited edition prints and posters are also available from the artist. She may be contacted at PO box # 4048, Palm Desert, CA 92260.

SHAMANIC WISDOM II:
The Way of the Animal Spirits

Dolfyn and Swimming Wolf

Earthspirit, Inc.
2103 North Decatur Road, # 135
Decatur, GA 30033

Table of Contents

The Way of the Animal Spirits

"When a man sought to know how he should live, he went into solitude and cried until in vision some animal brought wisdom to him. It was Tirawa, in truth, who sent his message through the animal. He never spoke to man himself, but gave his command to beast or bird, and this one came to some chosen man and taught him holy things. Thus were the sacred songs and ceremonial dances given the Pawnees through the animals. So it was in the beginning."

Chief Letakots Lesa

Just as Tirawa sent animals to the Pawnee bearing holy truths and sacred rituals, so today we can tap into our own source of divine inspiration with the aid of the animal spirits.

The native, shamanic peoples have long believed that the animal clans have great medicine powers that they will share with us if we have the wisdom to receive their teachings.

Humankind's alliance with the animal clan extends far back into the dim days of prehistory, and although this bond has been all but ignored in modern times, our relationship with the animal realm can be as powerful and as meaningful today as it was in the past. Indeed, there is now more than ever a need for humankind to reconnect with Earth Mother's elder children — the animals.

1

Because they preceded us and witnessed our own evolution, animals are considered by many tribal peoples to be our grandparents, and worthy of the same degree of respect and reverence due our human forebears. They hold all of the animal clans in high regard — equal, and in some ways superior, to humankind.

Yet most modern people consider animals to be less intelligent, less conscious, less important than ourselves. We, as a society, simply view them as pets to be pampered, laboratory animals to be exploited or food to be consumed.

Perhaps we would be more willing to call upon the medicine gifts of the animals if we thought more like the shamanic peoples and were not so arrogant in our view toward animals. After all, we have seen over the last few hundred years the destruction caused when we act without the wisdom and guidance of our animal forebears. We thought we could walk alone, without the guidance of grandmother Wolf, of grandfather Bear, of all the collective wisdom of our wise, ancient relatives. Now is the time for us to renew the ancient bond between ourselves and the animal clan, that our path may be guided and protected once again by their ancient earth wisdom.

Invoking Animal Spirits

Shamanic peoples call upon the energies of the animals they revere. We, too, can avail ourselves of the powers of these animals, or their entire clan, by a process called "invoking." Invoking can be understood as a type of prayer, a way to call the spirit of certain animals into ourselves.

The Way of the Animal Spirits

When we invoke, we are literally inviting the spirit of an animal to live in or near us so that we may share their medicine power. We are also, by invoking an animal spirit, praying to the entire species of that animal.

Animal spirits hold in their very being the collective consciousness and wisdom of their species. Therefore, animal spirits make excellent teachers, guides and helpers for humankind. When we invoke any animal we are calling on the wisdom of the entire species. For instance, when we invoke Wolf we are invoking the power, knowledge and experience of all wolves, those living and those who have moved on to the spirit world.

When we interact with the animals in this way we learn to see them and all of nature in an entirely new way. We come to appreciate and revere the wisdom and power inherent in all beings in nature. We humans have developed scientific, technological and analytic ability and power, but the animal spirits have other powers that are in some ways beyond our own. We can receive their guidance and be healed by their medicine gifts by invoking their powers into ourselves. Ant and Antelope, Bear and Beaver, Cat and Camel — all wait to impart the lessons learned through untold eons before humankind had even evolved.

A very simple way to invoke an animal spirit is to simply visualize and call upon it. For example, perhaps you need to become more adaptable and clever. You might visualize Fox and say something like, "Fox Spirits, I am calling to you. Live within me and fill me with your cleverness." Or suppose you want to invoke Camel for his stamina and endurance. You might visualize Camel and say something such as, "Camel Spirits, I am calling on you. Live

3

within me and grant me your endurance." Some people find it helpful to look at a picture or statue of the animal they are invoking. And when we are done invoking the animal spirits, we always give thanks to them for coming and for helping us.

We can also invoke animals by emulating their behavior as we are calling upon them. We do this to honor animals, to align ourselves with their energies and to graphically call to the animal spirits to come to us. You can move like an animal and make sounds like one as you invite them to fill you with their powers. For instance, you might prowl like Lion and roar as you invoke Lion Spirits or you might spread your arms and fly like Eagle. Or you might growl like Bear, move like Bear and then call upon the medicine power of Bear.

Here is an invocation you can use to call upon Wolf or, better yet, create one yourself:

Wolf Invocation

Wolf Spirits, I am calling on you.
Wolf Spirits, be here now.
I need your help to be loyal and free.
Wolf Spirits, live in me!

You can change this simple chant and use it for invoking any animal. You could call Eagle, for example, by changing the last two lines to, "I need your help to soar high and free; Eagle Spirits, live in me!" Or you could call Cat with, "I need your grace and mystery. Cat Spirits, live in me!" and so forth. Always give thanks when you are done.

It is not necessary that your invocations rhyme. A

very effective way to invoke is to visualize a nature being, breathe deeply and emulate that being while speaking simply in your own words. For instance, perhaps you are feeling tired and depressed. Few of the earth's creatures live their lives with such energy and vigor as Hummingbird:

Hummingbird Invocation

Invoke Hummingbird by visualizing Hummingbird and then breathing deeply. Close your eyes and become Hummingbird. Feel the wings at your shoulders beating with Hummingbird's inexhaustible energy... Ask the Hummingbird Spirits to enter you, to live in your heart, to enliven your limbs and lift your spirits... Breathe in deeply again and feel the small, unstoppable spirit of Hummingbird enter you, filling you with strength and energy... Thank Hummingbird when you are done.

One way tribal peoples invoke animal spirits is by adorning themselves as the animals they are inviting in, donning feathers and fur or painting their faces to resemble an animal and then dancing or moving as that being. We can do this, too. If this method appeals to you, you may want to use the following guideline:

Dancing In Animal Spirits

Begin by breathing deeply until you feel calm and centered. Then pray to the animal spirits, inviting them to live in and dance with you.

Begin to move spontaneously while shaking a rattle or drumming, playing a drumming cassette or while others

5

create a rhythmic beat for you. As you move, you can chant, sing, pray and focus on calling in specific animals to dance with and in you. You may start to visualize, feel, or in some way be aware of the animal spirit coming in to you. When you do, move and/or vocalize like that animal. Allow it to speak through you and with you.

You may become energized and filled with the presence of the animal you called upon. Or sometimes a totally different animal may come. Be receptive to whatever happens. Either way, you may move differently — with the grace and abandon of the animal — and feel differently, for you will be enlivened by, and on some level become one with, that spirit animal.

Try to really let go and let the animal spirit express itself through your dancing. Put down your rattle or drum if it hampers your full expression. You may find yourself moving and vocalizing sometimes as yourself, sometimes as the spirit animal.

When you feel your energies peaking, sit or lie down in the stillness and allow any messages from the animal to come through to your heart or your mind. Try and establish a dialogue with the spirit animal while you are in this energized, receptive space. The message will come in the form of feelings, body sensations, visualizations or ideas that "pop" into your mind.

When you have finished, thank the animal spirit for coming to you.

Our adornment doesn't have to be elaborate, nor our dances stylized for us to honor the animal spirits. For

6

example, instead of an elaborate bird costume, we can simply wear a feather and move as Hawk or Eagle to invoke their powers. Or we can draw on a set of whiskers to emulate cat, then move with cat's grace as we invoke her mysterious powers. When invoking an animal spirit, try to let yourself become caught up in the energy of that animal, feel it filling you to overflowing.

At first you may feel inhibited, but keep at it. Dance alone if you are shy. You will eventually discover the abandon that signals the presence and is one of the lessons of the animal spirits.

When you are more comfortable, you might want to dance in animal spirits with a group of people. The animal spirits enjoy interacting with each other in this way and such group dancing enlivens all participants.

A brief invocation consisting of heartfelt words is also called a prayer. We can always simply pray to the animal spirits and ask them to share their particular medicine gifts with us.

For instance, if you find yourself frightened, you might invoke Lion to enter your heart and fill you with his courage. Or if you are feeling aimless and unproductive, you might pray to Ant to give you a sense of purpose by saying something like, "Ant Spirits, live in me and fill me with the will to work."

Let us emphasize that these are only suggestions to help you get started invoking, praying, and relating to the animal spirits. You will soon discover that as you concentrate on inviting various animal spirits into your life, you will come to develop intuitive ways of your own for communicating with them. Animals will begin bringing you messages in your dreams and you will also find that messages and contact from the realm of the animal spirits begin to come to you spontaneously, in a variety of ways.

The main thing to remember about invoking is that you are simply calling upon, sharing with and becoming aware of the animal spirits. This is done by visualizing, calling to or moving like that animal, or doing anything else that helps you to identify with and emulate the animal you are invoking. Whatever methods work best for you are the ones you should use.

There are numerous ways to facilitate the invocation of the animal spirits. One way is to spend as much time as possible in wild and natural places. The wild places of nature are the best places to invoke animal spirits, but a quiet backyard will do, and an indoor place can be made more inviting to the animal spirits if we keep plants and pictures of nature inside. As your relationship with your helper grows, you will discover new and original ways to deepen and enhance the special bond that you share with animals.

You can further the process of learning the lessons of the animal spirits by undertaking the study of them and their world. They are always teaching just by being what they are, but too often we humans are slow learners — our eyes clouded, our ears stopped and our minds muddled by our arrogance. It is only when we approach the animals with humility as our ancient ancestors did forgotten eons ago, as we would any teacher who had great knowledge to share with us, that we are able to comprehend the lessons they have to teach. (If you want an example of this, notice how often the animals discussed in this book survive by cooperating with each other and with the natural rhythmes of nature.)

Each of Earth Mother's children has their own medicine power, a unique way of dealing with the challenges they have faced and overcome throughout the ages. The proof of this is in the fact that they are still here. In this book, we have tried, by examining what the ancient tribal peoples of the earth understand to be the medicine powers of certain animals, as well as the most significant and unique aspects of these animal's lives, to uncover abilities and attributes that could help us today as human beings in a modern, very unnatural world. This may seem strange until we consider that so many of the problems we face today are a result of turning away from the natural world, its elegant balance and intuitive wisdom.

Perhaps some of the solutions to those problems might be found if we would turn back to nature — get off the highways and walk the wooded paths again — and look to the animal cohabitants of this planet for the lessons they can teach us, treat them with the respect they have earned by their instinctive wisdom and the honor and compassion they are due as important members of Earth Mother's creation.

Finally, no book on amimal spirits would be complete without mention of the duties, as well as the joys, of those who would invoke and befriend these beings. The animal spirits are there to help you, so it is only right that you help them in return. For instance, we do not avail ourselves of Beaver's energies and then do nothing to protect Beaver and her environment. This is a two-way relationship.

And, of course, the best way you can protect all of the animal spirits is by lovingly stewarding Earth Mother. This planet is the animal's home, it is our home, it is our responsibility. One of the most important ways to thank and honor the animal spirits is to do your part to keep the wild places wild and green and clean. There is no more reverent act than to pick up a tin can or soda bottle from a littered beach, to replant trees on a deforested hillside, or to devote time and money to an animal conservation organization. Ceremonies have their important place, but service to the planet brings its own joy. And remember, when you are doing your part to preserve and purify our Earth Mother, the animal spirits will be working with you, will be living in you, and surely there can be no more sacred invocation than this.

The Way
of the
Animal Spirits

Animal Spirits, I am calling on you.
Animal Spirits, be here now.
I need your strength to be strong and free.
Animal Spirits, Live in me!

Ant

Ant was ancient when humankind first appeared on the planet. For eons humans have watched Ant tirelessly working beside the other members of her clan with uncanny cooperation and unity of purpose.

We can invoke Ant medicine wisdom to teach us how to build a sustainable society in an increasingly complex and overcrowded world. However, it does no good if we learn to work with each other if we neglect to work with Earth Mother, and here, too, Ant has lessons to teach.

Ant is more than a scavenger, surviving on bread crumbs and bits of leaf. She is a steward, carefully managing her resources. Wood Ant is known for her practice of herding aphids (a tiny insect) outside of the nest so that they can eat and then bringing them back inside the ant hole for safety. Ants "milk" the aphids for "honeydew," a sweet liquid produced by the aphids. Mediterranean Harvesting Ant stores seeds underground as reserves in the event of drought, and some types of ants even practice a type of farming where fungus is grown on chewed leaf material placed in special chambers. We must look to Ant, who takes what she needs from Earth Mother without destroying Her in the process, and apply this wisdom to our own technologies.

Call upon Ant medicine for patience, cooperation, the ability to work hard and harmoniously with others and the wisdom to steward our natural resources.

Antelope

Antelope can be found in many parts of the world, but whether she makes her home in a tropical forest or a desert, she travels the world lightly, silently, gracefully.

Antelope's unusually shy and silent nature is the perfect backdrop for her highly developed senses of hearing, smell and sight. She relies for survival on these gifts, a knack for utilizing her surroundings as camouflage, and her ability to leap and run. When Antelope spies an enemy in her vicinity she will immediately freeze. Her coloring blends in well with her surroundings, so if she stays perfectly still she probably won't be detected. If she lives in forest or woodland, she will lie down in the dense cover and remain motionless till danger passes. Even a baby antelope realizes the value of concealment. Hidden by its mother in tall grass or underbrush, a young antelope will keep still if a predator wanders into the area.

Antelope shares with us the discipline to be still and silent. We can invoke Antelope when we need help in developing a reflective attitude and a meditative state of mind. Her medicine gift to us is the peace of inner quiet. For it is in contemplation that we can hear our highest selves and tap the wisdom of the spirit realm.

Antelope's medicine is the wisdom to know when to remain still and when to take appropriate action. Invoke Antelope medicine to help you develop mystic awareness through silence, meditation and contemplation.

The Way of the Animal Spirits

Antelope Speaks

There is a time for silence
And stillness in the dark,
Waiting for the wisdom
That's hidden in your heart.

To know the time for hiding,
To know the time for hope,
And how to tell the difference
Is the gift of Antelope.

Armadillo

Dawn is coming and the fast-lighting sky finds Armadillo on her way home after a night of burrowing in search of whatever sustenance the earth might provide — insects, worms, perhaps the occasional tuber or mushroom.

The night has been kind, Armadillo's strong claws have uncovered much to eat, and now she makes her slow way to any one of several burrows with a full belly, ready for sleep.

But a sudden commotion warns that rest will have to be put off for a while. Something big and quick is close and getting closer fast. Armadillo's sensitive nose smells danger, so instinctively she rolls herself into a tight ball, the close-fitting plates of her armor forming one of nature's most unique and effective defenses.

The next few minutes, or hours, are a waiting game for Armadillo. Her attacker explores his spherical find with sharp intakes of hot breath, seeking in scent some clue to this strange prey. Claws and teeth scrape the bony plates but find no purchase.

Things seem to be getting worse when a frustrated paw begins to roll Armadillo about in a last effort to find some way to pry open this stubborn creature. Finally the rolling stops and the assailiant leaves to search elsewhere for more promising prospects of breakfast.

Slowly Armadillo unrolls herself and sniffs the air for traces of danger, but she finds only the sweet air of early morning. Once again, her armor has saved her.

The Way of the Animal Spirits

Armadillo is not a dexterous animal. The heavy shell which she carries through life robs her of agility and slows her gait to a crawl. Yet, this morning, after a night in which more elegant creatures came to the violent end of their graceful lives, Armadillo will sleep again in her warm grass-lined burrow, thanks to the armor on her back and the patience in her heart.

Armadillo's armor consists of bony plates covered with horn which grow from the skin. Few animals have been able to evolve such effective means of passive protection.

Armadillo's medicine power is that of protection in stressful situations, especially those times when the best defense is to mentally and emotionally go within yourself until the storm has passed. One of the beautiful attributes of Armadillo's defense is that she protects herself without harming others. Therefore, she is an excellent ally for those involved in passive resistance to injustice.

Armadillo also teaches us about setting boundaries. In times of stress, she simply closes herself around her soft underbelly in the midst of, yet away from, the world. Her thick shell is a powerful symbol of separation and delineation. We invoke Armadillo medicine when we need to learn how to set boundaries, how to put limits on how much of ourselves we will give to others.

Badger

Badger may not have Bear's great size or Tiger's powerful claws, but she is an aggressive fighter who is totally without fear. Her thick skin hangs loose from her body and is resistant to the bites of her enemies, and some badgers have the ability to squirt a foul-smelling substance at their attacker. But the thing that makes Badger such an effective warrior is her fierceness and persistence. Once Badger has bitten an enemy she will not let go. She hangs on firmly no matter what happens. It is no wonder that most animals go out of their way to avoid annoying Badger.

Invoke Badger whenever you need some of her indomitable warrior energy. Fearlessness and courage are the medicine powers Badger bestows upon those who ally themselves with her.

Call on Badger medicine when you feel you're having trouble making your visions manifest, for Badger teaches us never to let go of a dream. Badger's medicine wisdom reminds you that you are never defeated as long as you do not quit.

Few people realize that Badger is able to make friends and allies with other animals so that all will benefit. For example, Badger may be led to a bee hive by Honey Guide Bird. When the hive is located, Badger breaks it open so that both she and the bird can eat. Or Badger may form a hunting alliance with Coyote. Badger medicine wisdom teaches us to communicate with and form mutually beneficial relationships with a wide variety of beings.

Banded Mongoose

The Banded Mongoose clan was out foraging for food one day when suddenly Eagle swooped down from the sky and grabbed a terrified mongoose in his sharp talons; then Eagle flew into a tree to get a better hold on the struggling animal.

The entire mongoose clan ran to the tree and, with no thought to their own individual safety, began climbing the tree, chattering and harrassing Eagle, loudly demanding that their relative be set free immediately. Finally, seeing that this meal just wasn't worth the trouble, Eagle freed his prey, who gratefully scampered back to the safety of her clan.

It is extremely rare for any animal to actually rescue a family or clan member once they are captured by a predator, but Banded Mongoose will do this whenever she can. A Mongoose clan lives together in total unity and oneness. Mongoose medicine is about helping each other, fully committing ourselves to those we love and offering our most loyal selves to our friends and family. Banded Mongoose teaches us that we are safest and happiest when we form strong bonds of alliance and commitment with others.

We can call upon Banded Mongoose medicine to attract loyal friends, and to strengthen our own commitment to be a loyal friend. Invoke Banded Mongoose when a friend in trouble needs you and you need the courage and persistence to help. Banded Mongoose is also invoked for unity within a group and for group bonding.

Bat

During the day Bat sleeps hanging upside down. At dusk he awakens to spend the night careening through the sky in search of food, guided by echos. Many animals prefer darkness to daylight, but few live in a world so full of shadows. Like other animals who are comfortable in darkness, Bat's medicine powers include occult abilities, positive magic and psychic power.

Bat is the only mammal who can actually fly. Bat long ago evolved into the sky and we can follow him into our own free and open spaces once we break the mental bonds which hold us back. His upward evolution inspires us as we invoke Bat for the freedom to fly, to soar.

In order to live in caves and hunt at night, Bat had to develop a unique way of perceiving his dark world. He learned to judge the location of objects by emitting an ultrasonic sound and then measuring the length of time it took for the echo to return to him. Scientists call Bat's method "echolocation." Bat "hears" his way around; sound reveals Bat's shadowy world in a way that sight cannot.

When we explore the murky depths of our subconscious, of the mysteries, even of confusing personal situations, we must often develop our ability to "hear" the messages that our intuition sends us. We must learn to listen, to pay attention to those faint but meaningful impressions, to find new ways of understanding the world around us. Invoke Bat medicine for a heightened awareness of deep intuitive knowledge. Bat tells us to listen to the echos.

Bear

Bear has been feared and revered since time out of mind. Neanderthal people honored her by placing bear skulls on their altars.

Bear is honored by many North American Indian tribes who recognize that she possesses many medicine gifts. American Indians also realize that Bear is often a teacher and a spirit helper.

Tribes such as the Chippewa and Pueblo recognize Bear's great healing medicine. The shamans of these tribes costume themselves, dance and act like Bear to invoke Bear's healing power.

The Iroquois and Cherokee conduct Bear Dances in which they move and act as Bear in order to be better able to pray to the Bear Spirits for assistance and guidance. Labrador Eskimo shamans are granted their shamanic powers by the Great Spirit, who visits them at their initiation vision as Polar Bear.

Many of the primal peoples revere Bear and realize that their healers, shamans and spiritual leaders will derive great benefit for themselves as well as the tribe by a close connection with Bear.

In the winter, Bears in cold locales will find a den and go into a dormant state, eating nothing and living off their own fat till spring. Bear teaches us to go within when we have problems, to seek knowledge through meditation, and to search for hidden wisdom in our dreams. Serene contemplation, quiet introspection and calm meditation are

Bear's wise medicine gifts. Instead of running here and there for the answers to our deepest questions, Bear says, "Go within, be silent, be still and listen for the answers in the deep winter cave of the subconscious."

Bear's ability to go within a den, sleep for a long time when all outside is harsh and cold, and then re-emerge in spring to take up the joy of life once again gives Bear the medicine knowledge of rebirth and renewal. Invoke Bear for these powers.

Polar Bear lives in a cold, fierce and barren place, yet she is right at home on ice and in the frigid sea. Her thick white coat provides camouflage and protects her from the cold, as does an insulating layer of fat.

Polar Bear medicine wisdom is about adapting and surviving in a hostile environment. Many modern cities are as cold and barren to the spirit as polar regions are to the body. Invoke Polar Bear medicine to find and keep the warmth alive in your heart — anywhere, in any circumstances.

American Black Bear, (whose coat may be brown, white, blue or black), resembles a small Grizzly and dwells in the wild forest areas still left in North America.

Black Bear is extremely intelligent and can also be very secretive. Often it is better not to make your entire store of knowledge known; at these times you can call upon Black Bear to help you keep your secrets to yourself.

Beaver

Beaver is one of those animals whose behavior bears a striking resemblance to human activity. These similarities make Beaver's medicine power unusually accessible and meaningful to us. When we see Beaver grappling with many of the same problems that we face, and finding such resourceful and life-affirming ways to resolve these problems, we are assured that her medicine is strong and her counsel will be wise.

Beaver has long been admired as the most highly skilled engineer in the animal kingdom. Beaver lives in a sturdy lodge of mud, sticks and branches. Using simple materials found in her environment she constructs a snug home that will shelter her and her family from the elements and from predators.

When constructing her lodge, Beaver always makes sure to provide plenty of entrances and exits so as to never be trapped. We invoke Beaver medicine for the ability to develop alternatives and the wisdom to never trap yourself in any way.

Most people know that Beaver builds dams, but few realize that she also builds canals. These canals provide Beaver with a convenient way to swim from pond to pond. We can call upon Beaver to open up new channels of communication, to provide access to new ways of thinking and unexplored sources of wisdom. Beaver medicine helps us to widen our horizons and facilitates the passage of ideas not only between ourselves and others, but between our own conscious and subconscious minds.

Shamanic Wisdom II

The dams Beaver builds help the environment by fostering ecological diversity. The ponds she creates offer many species a place to build a shelter or a bountiful feeding ground. In short, Beaver creates many opportunities for a wide range of wildlife.

Beaver medicine teaches us to cultivate and appreciate the rich diversity that we find on our planet, and reminds us that Earth Mother is only rich and beautiful if we are willing to save all the different species from extinction. Invoke Beaver's power to instill Earth stewarding energies in our hearts.

One of the most timely lessons that Beaver teaches is one directed at breaking down outmoded gender roles. Although all the members of a Beaver family are involved in lodge and dam building, the female is the most diligent. Beaver kits are brought food by all the family members, but the male Beaver is the most diligent in this regard. Beaver can ease us all through getting over sex role stereotyping. Women who are developing their strong side and men who are developing their soft side can pray to Beaver for guidance.

It goes without saying that we should invoke Beaver anytime we are in the process of building, whether it be a home, a business, or a career. Beaver builds her structures one stick at a time, carefully choosing twigs and branches and then patiently weaving these materials together. Beaver helps us remember that any great accomplishment is the result of many small tasks faithfully and carefully executed.

Bee

She can be found in the early spring, darting from flower to flower, filling the world with an electric hum as if powerful currents of new life were vibrating the very air. Bee is not only a sign, but a source, of spring; a tireless helper in the happy work of pollenating the countryside. She was also the world's first confectioner, her honey a prized treat for many animals.

For one so closely associated with sex and sweets, Bee lives a surprisingly mundane life. Like Ant, she is concerned wholly with the work and welfare of her society. For Bee, the good of her society is largely the good of her Queen. The Queen Bee is cared for and honored by the rest of the hive because she is the mother of the entire colony. Thus, she serves as a symbol of the earth, our own Mother. Invoke Bee medicine to teach us to honor Earth Mother.

Bee's complex society couldn't sustain itself without excellent communication between its members. Bees exchange information in a variety of ways, such as intricate dances and complicated mathematical flight patterns. Therefore, many people invoke Bee medicine for communication.

Finally, one should always remember that, theoretically, Bee shouldn't be able to fly. She literally "flies" in the face of physics every time she visits a flower. But that doesn't stop Bee and it shouldn't stop you, if you really want to accomplish something, when people say that you can't. Possibility is an attitude. Impossibility is an opinion. Call upon Bee to help you do what can't be done!

Boar and Wild Pig

Wild Boar is among the most ferocious fighters that nature has produced. Her warlike attributes have been honored since antiquity. Many ancient warriors wore boar tusks on their armor to protect them in battle and to infuse themselves with her savage fighting energy. As recently as the time of King Henry III, boar emblems were used by soldiers to invoke Boar's medicine powers. Therefore, we invoke Wild Boar when we need courageous fighting ability for our own protection or for the protection of that which is dear to us.

Wild Boar is also invoked for fertility by many peoples the world over. This is because Boar produces many large litters of piglets who grow up healthy because they are all very well cared for. Tribal peoples the world over honor her wit and cleverness and also invoke these powers into themselves by calling upon Wild Boar.

Wild Pig ranges the forests and woodlands, hunting in a small band. She is very communicative with those in her clan, continually expressing herself with grunts, snorts and squeaks. She says a great deal by grunting in a variety of ways. For example, a loud, sharp grunt means, "Danger, run!" A series of softer grunts which sound like a chant means that courtship and love are in the air. Invoke Wild Pig for the courage to communicate your ideas and feelings even if you are not eloquent or poetic. She teaches us that whatever means of expression is available to us at the time is all that is necessary to express our truth.

Buffalo

"Across the circle from south to north we painted a red road, and Fox Belly made little bison tracks all along on both sides of it, meaning that the people would walk there with the power and endurance of the bison, facing the great white cleansing wind of the world. Also, he placed at the north end of the road the cup of water, which is the gift of the west, so that the people, while leaning against the great wind with the endurance of bison, would be going toward the water of life."

Black Elk

The Native Americans who for millennia walked the plains of this continent did so because of the power and endurance of Buffalo.

The great herds that covered the plains in the autumn like a vast, brown ocean were the source of the "water of life" to the people who respectfully, even reverently, obtained from Buffalo all they needed to sustain themselves. Buffalo provided food, clothing, shelter, even fuel; he was killed only when he was needed to support life, and then with gratitude and honor.

Buffalo also provided spiritual sustenance. The Lakota tell how White Buffalo Calf Woman brought to the people the sacred pipe, whose smoke was prayer made visible. Like the pipe, Buffalo medicine awakens the spirit to pray, to seek peace, to seek oneness.

Invoke Buffalo for these medicine gifts and also invoke him in order to bring to yourself the enormous bounty of the universe which is your birthright as a being who is a part of that universe. But always accept creations's largess with a feeling of respect and thankfulness in your heart.

Buffalo has served as a tragic example of what can happen to a species when humankind uses the bounty of Earth Mother in a wasteful, short-sighted, obscenely disrespectful manner. There were once as many as sixty million Buffalo in North America, but by the end of the nineteenth century they had been hunted almost to extinction.

Happily though, Buffalo's medicine power is not about extinction, but of survival, or, as Black Elk put it, of endurance. In this century, the Buffalo herds have returned, perhaps not as many as before, but enough to insure that Buffalo will be with us, that this source of the "water of life" will not go dry.

Call upon Buffalo for "power and endurance" when you "lean against the great winds" that blow through life from time to time.

Bull

We stand on the crest of a low hill. Around us a lush forest falls away from Earth Mother's back like a gown draped loosely about the shoulders of a queen. In this sunlit clearing a small herd of cattle graze, serene and milk-laden, interrupting their nibbling occasionally to watch as an ungainly calf struggles to master its new body. A breeze brings the smell of new grass and the sound of the cows' soft lowing. City tension drains from our bodies into the transforming earth and once again we find ourselves amazed at the many ways Earth Mother makes manifest the sublime.

Yet, nature spices Her every aspect with a paradox and provides Her every attribute with a protector. So it is now, for as we turn we meet the wild, warlike eyes that sired this peaceful herd; we behold the strength that guards these gentle ones. Standing before us is the bull of this group, his aggressive face peering from beneath thick, curving horns, knotted muscle growing like tree roots from hoof to shoulder and flank. Awesome, unchallenged, incapable of fear or surrender; is it any wonder he has been worshiped for millenia as a god?

First as adversary, then as admirer, humankind's relationship with Bull began in the Old Stone Age, when wild cattle were a major source of food for our struggling forebears. Bull was a mighty opponent for those early hunters, for he is a large animal — quick, powerful, with sharp, deadly horns. To successfully hunt and kill the more easily subdued females of a herd, one first had to deal with the bull, who protected his harem with great ferocity. Many an ancient hunter was wounded or killed in this risky process, and so a bull not only provided nourishing food and warm clothing, but also captured the imagination of humans as a symbol of the great warrior and fighter.

As these human clans slowly emerged from their caves to build cities and civilizations, they retained their reverence for Bull. In addition to his medicine powers of strength and power, Bull is recognized for the medicine gift of fertility, for he has the power to impregnate large numbers of cattle in his harem.

Many magical powers are attributed to Bull. Among these are the ability to bring thunder, storms and rain because, as he leads his large family thundering over the plains, he invokes powerful weather medicine by emulating the sound of thunder. The ancient Sumerians worshiped Enlil, the Bull god of storm and fertility. Through the medicine powers of Enlil there was water and all things were able to grow and flourish. Ancient India and Egypt worshipped fertility bull gods and, in Crete, Bull was invoked for passion, sensuality, fertility, power and sexuality.

Bull's medicine powers teach us courage and help us develop a fighting spirit. Bull can also be invoked for shielding and protection from negative energies by visualizing Bull standing in front of you, head down, horns ready, hoves pawing the ground. Not many negative energies would dare to trespass that forboding image!

Butterfly

Butterfly is the flower of the air, a vision of the opulence which overflows from every seam of creation. She is an infinite watercolor, painted by the Goddess and fluttering to earth in a trillion swirling beings.

When we consider Butterfly — her triune metamorphosis, her exquisite beauty, her otherworldly flight through springtime meadows — it isn't surprising that she has long been recognized and honored by the native peoples of the world as an emissary to the spirit world.

The Puma Indians told how the Great spirit took the shape of Butterfly and flew all around the world to find the best place for humans to live.

Some native peoples believe that when we sleep our soul assumes the shape of a butterfly and is then able to temporarily leave the body. We experience the freed spirit's flight as dreams. Therefore, Butterfly medicine is invoked for improved dream recall and for lucid, or conscious, dreaming.

But Butterfly isn't born the lilting creature that decorates the breezes, and her transformation serves as an inspiration to those of us who sometimes wonder if our hard efforts at spiritual growth and evolution will ever reap any rewards.

Butterfly begins life as a larvae, and at this stage of development does nothing much except eat. Finally, she withdraws and spins a cocoon around herself where, hidden in the silken darkness, she becomes the delicate-winged being we know as Butterfly.

Shamanic Wisdom II

How much this is like our own path, where early days of searching, reading, listening and feasting on new knowledge are followed by long periods of meditation and rumination, till eventually we discover that we are something more than we were, something better, something beautiful.

We call on Butterfly medicine powers for inspiration as well as help in our own spiritual development and we also invoke her medicine when we seek transcendence and transformation.

Like all beings who can fly, Butterfly is also associated with the element air, whose medicine gifts include clear thinking and inspiration. Invoke Butterfly medicine power for these attributes as well.

Butterfly Invocation

Gossamer being, soul in flight,
Free my spirit to fly the night.
Bringing dreams to set me free,
Butterfly Spirit, live in me!

Camel

Few animals know how to conserve resources better than Camel. His ability to endure the extreme heat of desert environments without having to drink water is legendary. Camel can go for up to ten months without drinking any water. He can also close his nostrils to minimize water loss as well as to keep out sand. When water is available Camel is capable of drinking up to thirty gallons of water in a very short period of time.

Another reason for Camel's amazing stamina is that he can go without food for a long period of time. He does this by storing fat in his hump and then living off that when food is unavailable.

Camel's medicine gifts are about endurance, conservation, economizing, patience, forbearance, stoicism, and the ability to survive when times are tough. Therefore, we can invoke Camel medicine for these attributes.

Camel only has to worry about conserving food and water because these are the only things he asks from the planet. We humans, on the other hand, have made many more demands on our earth, and it is obvious that the time has come when we must begin using our resources more conservatively and wisely.

Let us meditate on the medicine wisdom of frugal, careful Camel for inspiration and let us behave as he does when it comes to conserving Earth Mother's precious gifts. For if we do not, we will only make a desert of our beautiful, sacred planet.

Cat

To live with Cat is to live with a goddess. Genetically, Cat very much resembles her ancestors who roamed the savannah long ago, as she does her later-day cousins, the big cats, who live in today's jungles and wilderness areas. She has inherited the graceful movement and noble bearing of her forebears.

Cat is one of Earth Mother's most elegant statements of self — a molding in flesh of Her dignity, playfulness, power and mystery. We look into Cat's eyes, those lovely, inscrutable orbs that change phases like a pair of tiny moons, and know that behind them lie ancient secrets yet untold.

Many cultures down through the ages have recognized the divinity in Cat and have shown her great respect, even reverence. Bast, the Cat goddess of pleasure, joy, magic and sensuality, was worshipped in Egypt, where the punishment for killing a cat was death. When a cat died, the loss was mourned with burial rites and ceremonies. There were cat cemeteries where the sacred deceased were mummified and buried along with cat statues and other objects that they would need in the afterlife.

Egypt wasn't the only ancient society to look upon Cat as a diety. In Rome, the goddess Diana would on occasion take the form of a cat. In ancient Greece, Cat was associated with Demeter, a grain goddess, because Cat protects wheat from rodents. The Greek moon goddess, Artemis, is also associated with Cat; the ancient Greeks believed that Moon created Cat and Sun created Lion.

The Way of the Animal Spirits

Cat's lunar eyes that change phases, from crescent to round to crescent again, attest to her kinship with Moon. Therefore, cat can teach us to see with the Moonlight Vision, a sacred way of seeing that is psychic, intuitive, magical and wise. Ask Cat to help you see with Moonlight Vision by first gifting Cat in some way. For instance, you night help a stray cat or an organization that helps cats. There is no other animal as *quid pro quo* as Cat. That means Cat helps those who help Cat and Cat ignores those who ignore Cat.

During the burning times in Europe, when an estimated nine million women, healers, herbalists and priestesses were burned to death, Cat was associated with witches. These "witches" were actually practitioners of the "Old Religion," or Wicca, the ancient, pre-Christian shamanic nature religion of Europe. Untold numbers of cats were burned to death along with the wise women healers and priestesses.

The bubonic plague resulted when the cat population of Europe had been so reduced that the few remaining cats could no longer keep the rat population in check. This tragedy gives proof to the belief of many cultures that societies and individuals who honor Cat and treat Cat with respect enjoy good luck, but societies and individuals who mistreat Cat often have very bad luck.

Like Dog, Cat has joined her fortunes to those of humanity. But unlike Dog, Cat moved in on her own terms. She has the best of both worlds — the love and affection of a family and the freedom to live life pretty much as she pleases.

Invoke Cat medicine for independence, liberty, and

the ability to walk alone and yet find comfort, support and love. Cat's medicine powers also include grace, mystery and the ability to land on her feet. Therefore, we call upon Cat Spirits for these qualities. But psychic ability, insight into hidden mysteries and magical powers are the medicine gifts that Cat is consistently invoked for and appealed to by many peoples around the world.

If you are owned by a cat, you have probably noticed that Cat will join you whenever you meditate, do yoga, gaze into a crystal, read Tarot cards or engage in any otherworldly, psychic activity. The ancient Wiccans believed that Cat helped humans bridge the gap between the earth plane and the spirit realm. So do not shoo your cat away at these times, but realize that she is helping in all otherworldly endeavors.

Cat also posesses weather predicting powers. Folklore tells us that when she becomes wild and playful it will be windy; when she sits with her back to the fire there will be a hard frost or a storm; when she washes her ear it portends rain.

Folklore also attributes healing medicine to Cat. It is said that the tail of the Cat can touch various body parts for a healing effect.

Cheetah

She can be seen racing across the dry places of Africa and Asia, a graceful blur of speed and spots. Cheetah is the fastest land animal on earth, able to reach speeds of up to 60 miles per hour. Call on Cheetah when you feel like you are not making quick enough progress in any area of life. Her medicine gifts help us expedite any situation.

Cheetah's unique spine is one of the reasons she can run so fast. Her back is long and flexible, which allows her to make very long strides. Cheetah teaches us that often, when we want to speed things up, we need to stay very flexible as to the ways in which we accomplish our goals. We can't stay fixated on our original plan. Situations change, techniques change, even the goals change and we must change with them.

Whereas other cat's claws are covered by a sheath when retracted, Cheetah's claws are not, which gives her the traction she needs for rapid acceleration during a sprint. Nature has designed Cheetah so that she is always ready to run. Her medicine teaches us to always be ready, for much is either lost or gained in the beginning of any venture.

Cheetah is the fastest sprinter in the world, but has traded endurance for a short burst of speed. She only hunts on terrain that is open with just enough cover for her stalk. Cheetah says, "To be successful, know your strengths, know your weaknesses, and seek out environments that bring out your strengths."

We invoke Cheetah medicine when we want to accelerate our material or spiritual progress.

Coyote

He is born to the life of the desert. No generous trees drop coconut meat and milk at his feet, or offer a meal of bananas for the small labor of plucking and peeling. He doesn't move among rich foliage teeming with varied and nourishing prey. Instead, he forages for his food among the small bounty that the western American plains and desert grudgingly provide.

One might think that Coyote's life, lived in a bleak world of sand and cactus, Joshua tree and yucca, would be one of the more dismal existences on the planet. But Coyote has taken a stark landscape and transformed it with the infusion of one magical ingredient — the will to survive.

In Native American mythology, Coyote is the Trickster of the animal clan, a mischevious jester whose constant pranks are his way of affirming and celebrating life, no matter what the situation. His medicine is the power of an irrepressible optimism that he will be able to turn the bleakest circumstances into a winning situation. Coyote shows us the humor, adventure and paradox of life. He teaches us to laugh at the world and at ourselves. Coyote howls at the moon, he chuckles at the sun, and his dry desert home blooms with the joy of life that is in his heart.

Coyote is often honored in the legends of the Native American peoples, for he and they were close neighbors in the wide American west. But the reverence afforded Coyote was tempered with caution, for Coyote isn't above playing a trick or two on those who invoke him. Mischief is, by nature, hard to control, and there is no telling what Coyote will do. His tricks often get him into trouble, but in the end Coyote always lands on his feet.

Some legends say that Coyote is the Creator God of this world. It's not hard to see why people believe that Coyote, the Sacred Clown, formed this Earth Plane reality.

While most other predators of the world diminish, Coyote endures. His range is even increasing. Coyote is a success at life, because he does whatever he needs to do in order to survive. For instance, Coyote prefers to live only with his mate, but if hunting conditions are difficult, he will form a pack with other Coyotes so that they can all hunt more efficiently. Coyote has even been known to form a hunting alliance with Badger when it will benefit him to do so!

Invoke Coyote medicine when times are hard and you are having trouble seeing the way out of your problems, for the ability to develop alternatives is one of Coyote's many medicine powers.

Coyote's sacred irreverence allows him to know that the "authority" we ascribe to many hierarchies is unearned and misplaced. The bogus guru, the phony expert, the lying politician, the false prophets are all hilariously obvious to Coyote. Call upon him to help you see through the self-proclaimed "experts" who would have you pay them for the wisdom that is already yours. Perhaps these hucksters invoked Coyote themselves to sharpen their skills at fooling others! But people who do that find themselves tricked in the long run because, ultimately, Coyote's medicine power is life-affirming.

41

Shamanic Wisdom II

People who have had the child within crushed, who are too serious, too stuffy, or lack a certain sparkle, would do well to invoke a little Coyote into themselves. But, remember, a little Coyote goes a long way! His is a potent elixer and, like all of the most sacred and powerful medicines, a small dose is prudent.

People with a good sense of humor, an irreverent attitude, a penchant for mischief and a willingness to question all authority are especially dear to Coyote. He gives them a special kind of protection. Coyote isn't very good at keeping these folks out of trouble, because Coyote isn't all that good at keeping himself out of trouble. But he can be called upon for getting them out of it once they've gotten into it, though he often waits until after he has extorted his full measure of enjoyment at their predicament.

Coyote Speaks

Play and laugh and dance with glee.
The joke's on you, the joke's on me.
My way is truly sanity.

With trickster humor I do survive;
Through wit and laughter you, too, can thrive.
I am Coyote, and I say, "Come alive! Come alive!"

Crocodile, Alligator and Plover

Few beings seem to have been designed so exclusively for the task of survival as Alligator and Crocodile. We would hardly suspect them of a capacity for cooperation or caring but, as is often the case when learning about Earth Mother, things are more complex than they appear.

Crocodile's large teeth are an invaluable asset when hunting, but leeches often attack her gums. Therefore, Crocodile will come up to shore, open her mouth and wait for her ally, the Plover. This little bird hops into Crocodile's mouth and eats the bothersome leeches. Although Crocodile eats birds, she never harms Plover.

Besides getting rid of leaches, Plover also sounds a cry of alarm whenever Crocodile's enemies are near. In this mutually beneficial alliance, Crocodile insures Plover sustenance and Plover keeps Crocodile healthy and safe. We invoke Crocodile and Plover medicine to help us form alliances and to help us find positive ways to get along with people who are very different from ourselves. Crocodile medicine teaches us that we can find friendship where and with whom we least expect it.

Female Alligator guards her eggs carefully. If a baby has trouble hatching, the mother will take the egg into the water and gently crack it with her teeth. Her powerful jaws, so accustomed to dispensing death, can also serve as the handmaiden of new life. We invoke this aspect of Alligator when involved in efforts to redirect aggressive energies towards positive, life-affirming endeavors.

Deer

She moves delicately, almost unseen, the soft grey brown of her coat blending into the forest. Her attentive ears listen for hints of trouble and the huge eyes peer between dusty shafts of sunlight and moss-covered trees for signs of predators. She is truly among the most beautiful of the forest creatures, embodying the fragile grace shared by all those beings designed for silence and speed. To encounter Deer is to behold the soul of Earth Mother in Her most gentle aspect, a soft, almost unnoticed presence — magical, mysterious.

Deer is always on the alert for trouble, so when a dangerous situation arises, she can be gone in a flash, bounding through the underbrush in long, elegant leaps. Deer medicine teaches us to be immediately aware of anything that is detrimental to our emotional, physical or spiritual well-being and, if need be, to exit gracefully and quickly, before we are harmed.

You can call on Deer to inspire kindness, mildness and gentleness in yourself, for Deer teaches tenderness of heart and benevolence. Because they are so gentle, deer are thought of as timid, and this is true to a certain extent, but those who really know Deer know that she has a fierce side also. Male Deer are very belligerent with each other, fighting vigorously for females and for territory. This jousting is highly aggressive and results in a great deal of injury among the stags. Female Deer has her fierce side as well. She will provide more milk and nurturance to her sons than to her daughters so that her male offspring will develop the necessary bulk to hold their own when fighting with other bucks. She will jeopardize her daughter's survival to insure a son's health, because she knows that such ruthless decisions maximize the chances of survival of her bloodline.

We may be surprised that such lovely eyes as Deer's can look at the world in such a cold, calculating way. Deer says, "Do not be fooled by superficiality. There is a fierce power even to me, one of the most gentle of Earth Mother's children. Light of foot does not mean light of heart, for still I must survive, and I must struggle and fight for that survival as all Earth Mother's children must."

Every year Male Deer sheds his impressive antlers and grows new ones. Invoke Male Deer for the ability to cast off the old when the time is right, no matter how important, even irreplaceable, it appears to be.

Deer Speaks

My spirit gifts blend in a well-balanced brew —
The peace of soft power I grant unto you.
I'm light and dark shadow, fierce but still kind,
A measure of heart and a measure of mind.
Be ever alert, to see deep within.
Follow my hoof prints to know where you've been.

Dog

Perhaps they were a genetic mistake, perhaps another step in a divine plan so ancient that it had no beginning. But there they were, standing naked and terrified on the savannah, poorly equipped for life in the harsh world in which they found themselves. They were not large creatures, nor were they strong. They were not swift of foot, nor could they fly. They had neither fang nor claw, nor even warm fur to protect them from the elements. During the day they watched birds knit secure nests and beavers build strong lodges, but at night they huddled in caves they chanced upon in their wanderings — if they were lucky.

These hapless creatures were, of course, our own ancestors. How vulnerable they must have felt, with good reason, as they struggled to stay alive in a world filled with predators who could crush them with their great bulk or tear them with their strong claws and sharp teeth. How hopeless it must have seemed trying to catch a prey who could simply outrun them. And how they must have marvelled and rejoiced when one of the fiercest of these wild beasts stepped from his own world and extended a paw in friendship and fealty, offering to guide, protect, even love these new, hairless creatures with the strange habit of walking on two legs.

We'll probably never know what prompted this much needed offer of assistance, but no one can doubt that from that time till this, humankind has never had a more devoted friend in the animal realm than Dog.

The Way of the Animal Spirits

Dog has been honored and revered by many of the cultures which he has served. Much of this honor has been due to Dog's reputation and skill as a guide. Ancient Egyptians revered Dog as a guide to the underworld. They realized that just as Dog leads the blind on the earth plane, so do spirit dogs shepherd our souls when we pass on to the spirit realm.

Dog was also recognized by the Egyptians for his abilities as a spirit guard. Dog guards humans in this world, and protects human spirits who travel in other worlds, whether it be in vision quests and trance journeys, or on that final journey our culture calls death.

In ancient Persia stray dogs were honored as being akin to holy people who gave up home and security to wander the land and beg for food; consequently, stray dogs were fed and appreciated as sacred beings.

Folk wisdom teaches us that if a stray dog honors you by coming home with you, you are sure to have good luck. We can learn from this ancient wisdom that when we feed or help a stray dog we are granted luck and blessings.

Dog medicine is similar to Wolf medicine in many ways -- in their loyalty to family, for instance, and in their courage, heart and willingness to defend their territory. But the greatest lesson Dog can teach us is that of unconditional love. No child of Earth Mother has learned this lesson more completely.

Unconditional love is one of the strongest healing powers in the universe, and anyone who has been honored by Dog's friendship knows how well he administers this great medicine. Dog is a spiritual teacher to humans. He can heal our hearts and teach us what love and loyalty really mean.

Call upon Dog medicine to inspire you with the ability to love life and other beings unconditionally, for this is the highest of spiritual love.

Dog has thrown in his lot with humankind, trusting us, loving us, protecting us and asking nothing in return other than to share our lives. I view my own dog as my best friend and spiritual advisor, and I urge others to give back that love, that trust, by helping and feeding and caring for stray dogs. In this way we honor Dog, and we invite his powers into ourselves.

Dog Speaks

When the life of your forebears was risky and dire,
I guarded their backs as they sat by the fire.
Devotedly with you since time out of mind,
Four loyal feet always trotting behind.
And when your life's over my duties abide;
I'll be there to serve as your spirit's last guide.
For I have been sent by the star gods above
To bring you their gift — unconditional love.

Dolphin

Of all the creatures that walk, wiggle, fly, swim, crawl and hop across the face of the planet, none have a medicine power that is more badly needed by humankind than Dolphin. Nor is there any creature better able to understand our needs, anticipate our questions and articulate answers that will have meaning for us.

Though she is a water being, Dolphin is, like us, a mammal; she is also the most intelligent animal on the planet. Her friendliness towards humans has been well documented, as have her numerous attempts to communicate with us. Dolphin has many things to teach humankind, and she is fairly easy to invoke, because Dolphin knows how desperately we humans need her great wisdom.

The lessons Dolphin has to teach concern the hidden, nebulous, right-brained mysteries that we seem to have forgotten. Humankind chose to explore the mysteries of the land and of Sky Father. Dolphin, on the other hand, never left Earth Mother's vast womb, but chose to stay in her moon-rippled ocean, swimming out the eons, content to make her home in the mysterious element of water. She made no tools and she built no cities, for she knew that to simply live life fully and happily is accomplishment enough. Dolphin realized that to simply hold one's place in the circle, to be one golden link in the chain of life, is the highest goal to which we can aspire.

Most Dolphins have a very free and open social organization. The members come and go as they please. For those who wish independence without loneliness and freedom in community, there is no better guide for this than Dolphin.

Dolphin is the essence of connectedness and interrelatedness. She teaches a kind of love that, once felt, is startling in its power, irresistible, even humbling. Dolphin has created a society where unconditional love is a birthright, precious though ever present.

Invoke Dolphin medicine for the secrets of the deep, hidden mind of Earth Mother. Most importantly, invoke Dolphin for her love and for the miracle of healing made possible by that love.

There are places where people pay a fee to swim with Dolphins. The Dolphins are extremely loving and protective of the handicapped children who are brought there for therapeutic purposes. Often only one session is needed for great transformational healing of the spirit to take place. However, it is neither necessary nor right to hold Dolphins captive. These beings are at least as intelligent as you and I and have at least as much right to their freedom. (No animal was created by the Great Spirit to be locked up or caged.) Besides, we can allow Dolphin to transform and heal our spirits simply by invoking her.

Invoke Dolphin medicine for wisdom, understanding, intelligence, enlightenment, playfulness, joy, unconditional love, flow, balance, harmonious relationships, communication and social awareness.

Dove

Dove has been recognized by people throughout the ages for a variety of medicine gifts, but the most important of these by far has been that of romantic love. The Greeks associated Dove with Aphrodite, the goddess of Love, and the Romans depicted Venus, their love goddess, as riding a chariot pulled by doves.

This association with love is obvious because of Dove's tender courtship, monogamous relationship and dedicated parenting. Indeed, Dove seems to have been created for romance; the male dove begins his gentle cooing before he is even fully grown. When he has found a prospective mate, he will court her by cooing, bowing, dancing and nuzzling her with his beak. Doves will often spend hours running their beaks through each others feathers, with the male doing most of the preening while the female enjoys the attentions of her beau. The courtship phase can go on for quite some time and, once mated, doves stay together for life.

Dove is invoked for love, romance and loyalty. Dove medicine teaches us to be more tender with those we care for. Dove is also recognized by many diverse peoples as a bird of peace, prosperity, purity and spirit.

Although Dove has captured the imagination of people since time immemorial, we should also honor Pigeon as well. Dove and Pigeon are closely related and have basically the same lifestyle and abilities. Invoke either one for their many medicine gifts.

Eagle

Since time immemorial, Eagle has been worshipped and revered by many different peoples for his medicine powers . Native American Indian tribes recognize Eagle as a spirit bird with strong medicine who, because he flies high and is at home in the heavens, is one with the Great Spirit who lives in the sky. That is one reason Eagle feathers are considered an important healing tool of many native healers or shamans.

Native peoples of this continent have traditionally relied on Eagle's courage to help them through the demands of their tribal initiation. We can also invoke Eagle medicine when facing difficult challenges, for it is said that those who honor Eagle and follow his ways will be given a gift of courage, endurance and fortitude. Eagle medicine wisdom teaches us to overcome and ultimately conquer the boundaries of this world.

But Eagle medicine also helps us cross the boundaries into other realms. Eagle is known for his ability to help us in developing shamanic powers, among them soul traveling or spirit journeying to alternate worlds. Invoking Eagle fills us with the ability to soar to great spiritual heights and leads us swiftly and surely to the spirit realm where all things are possible.

Because Eagle is such an integral part of the heavens, it is not surprising that he has long been associated with Sky Father and the sacred solar power of transcendence. With Eagle's eyes we can see with the Sunlight Vision,

The Way of the Animal Spirits

whose brilliant light sharply illuminates the truth against the murky backdrop of illusion. This clear vision enables us to see far, to view our own life and our mundane cares and worries from a new perspective, thus allowing us to fly far above these limiting details, focusing on that which is most important — developing our spirits.

In ancient Babylonia, Eagle was identified with Lagash, god of thunder, storm, war and fertility. Many divergent cultures recognize Eagle as a Thunder Bird and associate him with powerful storms, for he is brother to the Cloud Spirits and is revered for the strong, swift flight that allows him to soar freely among the clouds. In ancient Rome, Eagle was invoked for protection from lightning.

The ancient Hindus revered Eagle as the bringer of soma, the sacred plant used to induce transcendent and ecstatic states of consciousness.

We invoke Eagle medicine for clear vision, illumination, transcendence, the ability to see far and the freedom to fly high.

Finally, Eagle, who spends much of his life experiencing the joy of flight, represents freedom, independence and untamed energy. Perhaps this unfettered joy of living is why he is such a long-lived bird, and why rejuvenation, renewal and longevity are also considered to be some of the medicine gifts of Eagle.

Elephant

They padded slowly down the path towards the place of the old ones, a mother elephant and her calf, come to commune with their grandmothers. The path and the burial ground had been tucked into this forgotten corner of the jungle for centuries, the former used for the many comings and goings of the elephants life, the latter of use when that life was over.

As they approached the burial ground the memories began. The great mother elephant slowed her pace as faint impressions moved like mist through her brain — the taste of strange bark, mud of a color never seen before, the frightened skin of night travel.

These were not her memories but the memories of these resting souls. The love and lessons of a hundred generations littered this sacred spot amid the chunks of broken bone and cracked ivory.

The young one could feel the memories too, though she couldn't comprehend their meaning. She could only move a bit closer to her mother, as if asking for an explanation of this new knowledge, this ancient love.

But her mother was engaged in her own search for understanding as she stood quietly contemplating the bleached bones and yellowing tusks that lay scattered through the clearing like a divination cast by a god. And, in fact, here was an oracle, the source of the visions and the light of the dreams.

The Way of the Animal Spirits

Slowly the mother began to sort through the bones, gently exploring, prodding, finding here and there a clue to the mysteries elephants ponder, answers to the questions they ask.

When she had gleaned her bit of wisdom, she called her calf to her and together they left the clearing, trudging back to the present, borrowed visions fading like morning's last dream. The old ones and the memories wait patiently for their return.

Elephant helps us get in touch with the collective subconscious memory of our ancestors. Just as Elephant visits the burial grounds of her forebears to stand in silent contemplation, so does she help those who emulate her to rediscover ancient memories, including our previous lives on earth, through dreams and meditations.

Elephant is one of those animals that Earth Mother made to encourage us to look beyond the surface of Her creation, to search for the surprises and the paradoxes that She has hidden in nooks and crannies throughout the planet.

No one can look at an elephant without being aware of an intimidating physical presence, the great size, the unequaled strength. But few would guess at the sensitivity of this animal, the delicacy with which elephant moves and maintains her huge body.

And who would know (unless they had looked deep into those eyes) that somehow inside that huge head and heart Earth Mother has placed for safekeeping a goodly part of Her own spirit. Elephant guards and grants the ancient and subtle blessing of matriarchical wisdom. She teaches this knowledge by act and example. Elephants live in close knit groups that are led by the oldest female, who understands and guides her clan through the crossroads and changes of life, the deep mysteries of birth and death. Hold Elephant in your mind's eye; visualize the old matriarch leading her clan to water. Ask for her guidance in your life, that she may grant you the wisdom to lead.

Elephant's leadership would serve as a good example for our own officials. She uses her strength to protect her charges, not to dominate them. When danger approaches, the clan huddles together with the young at the center and the matriarch facing the danger.

A strong love exists between members of an elephant clan. They live together harmoniously, each looking after the other, all looking after the young. If one elephant is hurt, all of the others will come to help, no matter the danger. Elephant inspires altruistic, selfless love and courage. Call on her to invoke family unity and strengthening of family ties.

Elephant follows the same paths over many generations to make Elephant roads through dense jungles. We can invoke Elephant when we want to develop a sense of tradition and explore the paths of wise ones who went before. We invoke Elephant when we want to get in touch with ancient paths and knowledge.

Elephant has a fine memory and an excellent ability to learn. Call upon her to enhance memory, studying and intellectual achievement.

Elephant is well known for her long life span. Many people believe that invoking Elephant can promote longevity, health and good luck.

The Way of the Animal Spirits

Elephant Speaks

I walk the wide savannah
As the wind blows through the grass.
The sounds are words of wisdom
Whispered to me from the past.

My trunk dips to the river
And I taste the cooling stream.
The water's a reminder
Of a time preceding dream.

I move slowly through a jungle
That has grown up on the bones
Of my mothers and my sisters
So I never walk alone.

I hold for you the history
That has passed before these eyes.
Call on me for counsel
And the memories of the wise.

Fox

Fox has long had a reputation as a clever and crafty survivor, adept at utilizing whatever resources happen to be at hand and extracting the maximum advantage from every situation. His adaptability can be seen in the great variety of food he consumes. Fox eats what is available in his environment. If he lives in a coastal area he will dine on whatever the ocean provides, timing his visits to the beach to coincide with low tide so he can easily gather the food that washes ashore. If Fox lives in an area rich in fruit, then 90% of his diet will consist of fruit. Call upon Fox medicine to help you glean ample spiritual and physical nourishment wherever you are, in whatever circumstances. Fox grants to all who invoke him the medicine power he holds in abundance: cunning, adaptability, wit and cleverness.

Fox doesn't always consume his food at one sitting, but will store foodstuffs away for future use. Fox rarely forgets where his caches are hidden. These are some of the reasons that people from many cultures invoke Fox energies for the gifts of good memory and intellect that serves practical purposes.

Fox is always alert for any danger and every opportunity, reacting quickly to every new situation. Invoke Fox medicine when intelligent and decisive action must be taken on the spur of the moment. And just as Fox stealthily moves through his habitat, all but invisible, so his medicine wisdom, when called upon, inspires us to blend in harmony with the wild places of nature.

Frog and Toad

Frog and Toad are not usually revered as magical beings in modern European-based cultures, but wiser civilizations have recognized their magic and honored their medicine powers, especially those concerning love, fertility and childbirth.

Frog is sacred to Venus, the Roman goddess of love, and the Babylonians used Frog seals for fertility charms. The Egyptians associated Frog with Hecate, goddess of childbirth. This isn't surprising, considering the variety of ways Frog and Toad have found to safely hatch their eggs. For instance, the Midwife Toad leaves her eggs with the male, who carries them on his legs until they hatch. Some frogs lay their eggs in foam nests suspended over a stream or pond so that the newly hatched tadpoles can drop safely into the water. In these and other creative ways, the survival of an adequate number of the young are assured.

With fertility has come variety, and few creatures have managed to find a niche in as many different environments as Frog and Toad. There are many species of frogs and toads, each one more interesting than the next. The sheer creativity, imagination and diversity of these fascinating creatures has earned Frog and Toad an honored place in the cultures of many peoples. While many frogs are happy to stay near the water, others have left the marshes for different and dryer homes. Some frogs live on the forest floor and lay their eggs in plants or in holes in the ground. Other frogs have taken to the trees, developing suction cups on their feet so powerful that they can cling to any surface, even vertical glass. Flying Tree Frog even ventures into the air, gliding from tree to tree by using the membranes on her feet to navigate. These are just a few of the reasons we call upon Frog and Toad medicine to open our minds to creative alternatives, to show us unique and unorthodox approaches when faced with a challenging situation.

Male Frog sings to attract a female. Frog's song is associated with the coming rain, for most frogs and toads must lay their eggs in a moist environment. Therefore, Frog is invoked during droughts to bring forth the rain.

Frog and Toad are also invoked by some societies for the ability to change and grow because of their transition from egg to tadpole to adult.

Frog and Toad are recognized by many peoples as magical beings and are invoked for their ability to grant magical powers.

Folk wisdom informs us that dreaming of Frog means that you will have good fortune and if Frog visits your home you will be blessed with romantic love.

Frog and Toad medicine bring rain, abundance, fertility and creativity. Therefore, when you see or hear Frog or Toad, immediately stop, close your eyes and visualize abundance for yourself and for all life. Then give thanks to Frog and Toad for calling forth the healing, life renewing rain.

Giraffe

Giraffe is one of the most successful and widespread vegetarians of the African savannah. Her long neck is a unique gift that quite literally allows her to reach for the heights, to eat the vegetation that her shorter competitors can't reach. Therefore, we invoke giraffe medicine when we want to reach for the heights, to set our sights on a goal that some might think is beyond our grasp. Giraffe is also invoked for individuality and for success in creatively and imaginatively solving problems.

Hearing and smell are quite keen in Giraffe, but sight is her most acute gift. From the lofty vantage point provided by her height, Giraffe can see clearly far into the distance, and is aware of approaching predators or distant feeding grounds. Invoke Giraffe medicine for clear vision and perspective in seeing ahead and anticipating what is next.

Giraffes bring their young to places known as calving grounds. These are areas used over and over again as places for the young giraffes to meet and form groups for mutual protection. Giraffe understands that when we are vulnerable, as the young calves are, we may need to be with others like ourselves, or sympathetic to us, for protection. She teaches us that when we are in a vulnerable place, or when something new and delicate is aborning within us, it is wise to find a safe place and nurturing people to be around.

Goat

Goat is a climber, always moving towards the summit. This is where he is happiest, and the wisdom to get there is his medicine power. He does not stumble. He offers a grounded, sure-footed wisdom to those who honor him. Whether his path is an easy one requiring only a skillfully placed hoof, or a difficult one filled with obstacles that must be butted out of the way, goat will persistently strive to attain his goal. If impediments absolutely cannot be butted aside, goat will simply leap effortlessly over his difficulties, land lightly and continue on his way. We can invoke Goat medicine for these abilities.

Goat also has a humorous, even mischevious side, and the ancient shamanic peoples of Europe honored his earthy, lusty aspects. They revered Pan, the woodland god whose bottom half resembles a goat while his upper body is that of a man. Pan is a joyful, lusty god who loves to play his flute while frolicking in nature. When the dominant, conquering religion "converted" the pagans at swordpoint, they tried to remake Pan into the image of the Devil, largely because of Pan's hearty endorsement of physical love.

Goat medicine is about sensuality and sexuality, and his wisdom is honored by those who cherish life's joy and ecstacy, revel in its mischief and passion. There are those who still hear the lively music of a magic flute playing in the wild places. They still dance to Pan's ancient tune, whether or not they know the name of the Goat God that still wanders the untrammelled woodlands of the earth.

Gorilla

Gorilla is the largest of the primates and genetically very closely related to humans, and so his medicine power is uniquely suited to human needs. When we look into Gorilla's eyes and listen to his medicine teachings, we are looking into our own ancient soul and hearing our own early wisdom, imparted first hand at the knee of Earth Mother in long-forgotten forests and in savannahs warmed by a new sun.

Gorilla is an extremely powerful being, but he is also very gentle, the jungle's teacher of serenity, tolerance and inner peace. He rarely causes physical harm, but he will assert himself by beating his chest in an impressive exhibition of power. The purpose of this display is to settle differences without getting physical. This is Gorilla's medicine gift to those who call upon his energies — to be gentle and mild, unless provoked. And then to express and assert one's position with drama, energy and power.

Gorilla is most loyal to his group of family and friends and yet he does not put his energy, as do most other animals, into territorial defense. We can meditate upon Gorilla's continual quest for peace and invoke him to help direct peaceful energy towards any situation.

In his wisdom, Gorilla never strips an area of vegetation when he feeds. He leaves some of it to regrow. Gorilla's wisdom can be called upon to inspire us to caretake Earth Mother so that we use Her resources wisely and in a life-supporting manner.

Grouse

Grouse Medicine is concerned with the celebration of the circle. Black Grouse, while putting on his courtship display for the female, dances in a circle. His quick, stylized movements remind us of the tribal peoples all over the world who have for eons danced the sacred circle, regarding it as the centerpiece of their spiritual life. Grouse medicine teaches us that the circle still has an important place in our spiritual practices today.

The circle is humankind's most ancient symbol of wholeness and perfection. It symbolizes Earth Mother in her fullness, roundness and abundance. Most tribal peoples perform their ceremonies and raise medicine power within a sacred circle, sometimes called a medicine wheel. The circle's shape evokes a sense of completion and endlessness. It speaks of the cycle of the seasons and the great wheel of birth, death and rebirth, reminding us that there is no death, no beginning, no past and no future in the spirit realm. We can invoke Grouse medicine for an understanding of the transformation and increase of power that occurs in energies swirling in a sacred circle or medicine wheel.

Ruffled Grouse is known for a drumming noise that he makes with his cupped wing. Drumming is also an ancient practice among primal peoples, used for communication over long distances, to keep time for dances and to induce trance and other states of altered consciousness. Invoke Ruffled Grouse medicine whenever drums are being used to raise energy.

Hawk

Hawk flew from the open hand of Sky Father into the high domain of the Wind Spirits, where smooth rivers of cold air slowly molded her into the Bird Clan's finest hunter. Hawk is blessed with a pair of powerful wings and the ability to fly well at great speeds. Because she is such a skillful flyer, Hawk can take her prey on the wing, on the ground or in the water. Her maneuverability in the air is so precise that she can pursue her prey through bushes and trees by closing her wings and steering with her tail, even to the point of flying into burrows or holes in trees.

Hawk is a great hunter who seizes her prey with sharp talons. Those of us who hunt and quest after food for the spirit are also great hunters, seeking to grasp an elusive spiritual prey with our hearts and minds. Hawk feels a kinship with those whose goals are spiritual. Pray to Hawk to speed all seeking and hunting, for she will teach our spirits to soar and fly with ease.

Everyone is familiar with Hawk's excellent eyesight. She floats far above the surface of a hunting ground that bustles with life and with illusion. She must decide before she dives whether a shadow flitting across the ground is a leaf blowing in the wind or a much needed meal. Hawk doesn't want to waste her time searching for sustenance where none exists, and neither do we want to chase after illusions and false hopes. We invoke Hawk for the perspective to see clearly and choose carefully from among the surfeit of choices in today's world.

The Way of the Animal Spirits

Hawk's medicine gifts are many. All of the Bird Clan are messengers to the Great Spirit, but Hawk is one of the most important messengers for she is the greatest of the flyers. Just as Hawk can travel from earth to the heavens to relay invocations and prayers from the earthbound, so can she bring guidance and comfort back from the heavens.

Those who honor, meditate upon and invoke Hawk can facilitate communication with the spirit realm. Pray to Hawk to open you to spirit knowledge and clear inner visions. When you see a hawk, raise your arms to her and call out your prayer. She will quickly deliver your message to the Great Spirit. Or just wait, quietly watching Hawk for a while to see if she has a message for you. The first idea, feeling or image that pops into your mind is probably a message from the Great Spirit, brought to you by Hawk.

The ancient Egyptians thought of Hawk as more than just a messenger. They looked upon Hawk as the representative of that part of the soul, called the *ba*, that could fly out of the grave after death. They even put narrow tunnels in their graves so that the ba could escape. Call upon Hawk medicine for the power to temporarily flee the confines of the earth plane when the burdens of this life threaten to smother your soul.

Hawk medicine is also about transcendent vision. Just as Hawk circles high above the earth to get a wider view, so do our spirits need to soar in order to bring a more universal wisdom to our lives. Therefore, we invoke Hawk for help in all spiritual pursuits that lend themselves to transcendent vision, such as vision quests, meditation and so forth.

Hippopotamus

Hippopotamus divides her life into two distinct sections; daylight hours are spent immersed in a watering hole or river, and nights are spent on dry land foraging for food. Hippo's skin tends to lose moisture quite easily, therefore she must spend most of her waking hours immersed in water.

The element of water is associated with deep feelings, inner knowing and intuition, and the element earth is associated with grounded practicality and mundane stability. Since Hippo is completely at home in both of these elements, her medicine powers are about being in touch with intuition, psychic abilities, emotions and sensitivity while at the same time staying grounded, practical, stable and pragmatic.

Life's necessities come rather easily to Hippo, who only has to graze about five hours during the night to adequately feed herself. The remainder of her day is devoted to resting in the water, so most of her life is spent lolling about, relaxing and thoroughly enjoying herself in watery bliss.

We can invoke Hippo medicine for the ability to finish our work quickly and efficiently in order to have plenty of time for rest and relaxation. Hippo medicine is about meeting our needs quickly and then spending most of our time enjoying life.

As evening approaches the hippo clan leaves their watering hole and ambles down the same trail that they have always used, to the familiar grazing area where they eat their fill. Hippo likes to keep to traditional ways and walk the path of her ancestors. Those of us who would call upon ancient wisdom and knowledge, who look to the old ways, can meditate on and draw inspiration from Hippo.

Hippo is extremely protective and nurturing towards her young, who often lie on her back in deep water when very young. That is why native peoples who live in Hippo's locale view her as a protective spirit and invoke her medicine for protection.

Hippo forms a variety of alliances, friendships and relationships with many other animals. For example, Cyprinid Fish keeps Hippo's skin free of algae. Birds like Stork and Egret will use Hippo's back as a perch when fishing. And Oxpecker (a bird) rides along on Hippo and keeps her skin free of insects and other parasites. Even young crocodiles will climb Hippo's back to bask in the sun and relax.

Hippo teaches us to get along easily with everyone, even those quite different from ourselves. We can invoke Hippopotamus medicine for tolerance, easy going amicability, a live-and-let-live attitude and the wisdom to help others whenever possible, for in doing so we help ourselves as well. Hippo medicine wisdom teaches us that all species on earth are interconnected, for are we not all children of our sacred Earth Mother?

Horse

Horse, like Dog and Cat, is one of those animals who has made an alliance with humankind. For thousands of years Horse has helped us to carry our burdens, grow our crops, travel our roads, even fight our wars.

One of the most striking things about Horse is a dignity that is impossible to diminish. Even pulling a plow or bearing the meanest burden, Horse maintains a noble bearing. Horse has shouldered his burdens without surrendering his essential nature. Even after his thousands of years of servitude, when let loose to run wild Horse becomes in a very short time the untamed spirit he was destined to be. Perhaps this is Horse's greatest medicine, the knowledge that no matter what we have borne in the past, there always exists in us the waiting seed of our true selves. Horse shows us how to carry our burdens with ease and with dignity, but more importantly, he shows us that we are always and forever free.

The first thing one notices about Horse is his impressive size and physical power. He is among the biggest and strongest of the animal kingdom, especially among those animals who have close interaction with humankind. Horse medicine teaches us how to tap our own inner power and use it to enrich our lives whether that energy is used to run across the plains kicking our heels in joy and celebration of life, or to pull a plow while growing food to sustain life. Invoke Horse medicine for personal empowerment, for accessing your own power.

The Way of the Animal Spirits

Horses are very socially oriented and live in relatively permanent herds. Normally among animals who form stable groups the males will, upon reaching maturity, strike out on their own while the grown daughters will stay in the mother's clan. But horses, both male and female, will leave the security of home to find, or form, their own herd. Invoke horse if you haven't yet gained complete independence and need to stand on your own feet now that you are an adult. Horse medicine helps us to find our own place in the world.

A newborn horse gets up and is moving about an hour after it is born. Whenever we begin something new, we are starting a learning process, like the new colt who is trying to use his legs for the first time. And like the colt, we are unsure of our footing and will wobble at first on shaky legs. This initial experience is the hardest part of any new project. But if we persist in our efforts, we'll soon be galloping towards our goal. Therefore, we invoke Horse medicine to get us through the early stages of new learning.

Who has not gazed in awe at the beauty of Horse in motion? Anyone who has ever ridden a horse knows that when he is trotting it is almost impossible to stay in the saddle. But when we allow the horse to set his own pace and he begins to gallop, then riding becomes a pleasure. We become one with the horse in an easy undulation across the plains. Horse teaches us that when we give our heart and soul full rein and let our spirit find its own rhythm, then we will ride through our lives with beauty and grace.

71

Hummingbird

Hummingbird is among the most beautiful of all the bird clans, with a wide variety of feather colors and patterns among the different species, whose plumage is heightened by a startling iridescence.

Hummingbird has long been associated with love, because no bird embodies so many of love's highest attributes — grace, beauty, delicacy, strength, passion — and because Hummingbird is, like this most intricate of emotions, a bundle of paradoxes. Tiny, yet tough, delicate looking but strong, Hummingbird has a grit and an aggressiveness far beyond anything her outward appearance would indicate.

Perhaps the most impressive display of Hummingbird's passion is in the male's glorious courtship flight for the female, who watches while perched demurely on a branch. After mating, the female will patiently construct one of the bird clan's most delicate nests, made from nature's finest materials. One species of Hummingbird even uses spider webs to construct her nest!

We can invoke Hummingbird medicine for knowledge of the heart and for passionate love. We can also call upon Hummingbird's grace, beauty, strength and delicacy for blending the conflicting passions and emotions of which love is composed.

Hummingbird is also associated by many peoples with joy and luck. Whenever you see a Hummingbird, stop and invoke her energies for good luck, love and happiness.

The Way of the Animal Spirits

Or simply visualize Hummingbird and then ask the Hummingbird Spirits to grace you with these medicine gifts.

Hummingbird's flight is a graceful aerial ballet. Because her wings beat so quickly, vibrating up to fifty times per second, she has a very precise control in the air. She can fly forward, backwards, up, down and sideways. And that is why Hummingbird medicine is invoked to open the heart and the mind to move in new directions when new situations demand a change of course.

Hummingbird darts from flower to flower in her search for nectar, seeming to lightly kiss the petals before moving on to another blossom. She teaches all who honor her to let in the beauty of life, the nectar of love.

Hummingbird is a tiny bird that consumes only flower nectar and insects. One would think that such a small and specialized bird would be quite fragile, but Hummingbird is surprisingly tough, even aggressive, often driving away larger birds. She survives in environments ranging from the desert to snow-covered mountains. One way she does this is to be constantly on the move for new sources of food, sometimes migrating thousands of miles seeking nectar and favorable living conditions.

Hummingbird medicine wisdom shows us that size is no indicator of strength or survivability, that our power comes from the spirit within us. She also teaches us the importance of timing, of being in the right place at the right time to find the things we need. We invoke Hummingbird medicine for romantic love, indomitable energy and the ability to tap great power from within.

Kangaroo

The joey (young kangaroo) looks out at the world from the warmth and safety of her mother's pouch. She finds herself at the edge of a thin stand of trees where underbrush and saplings share the land with fields of high grasses. Above her, her mother chews a mouthful of that grass, relaxed but alert, searching with nose and ears for any hint of danger. They live in a harsh environment, especially when the sky is stingy with its rain and the world turns dry and brown. But somehow the mother manages to find enough food to keep herself and her joey alive and, should the need arise, can quickly get them out of harm's way with a quick burst of strength from her powerful legs.

As she gazes at the world, contented and secure, there comes from somewhere deep inside the youngster a half-formed memory of an earlier time when, newborn and barely formed, she crawled up her mother's belly to nurse in the pouch where she now rests. She lives again the feelings of being exposed and defenseless in a world of which she knew nothing, and remembers the feeling of safety as she finally reached the pouch.

Now the slow months of maturation are drawing to a close and she will have to leave the pouch for good, to forage and fight for herself and, soon, for her own little one; again she will be young and vulnerable, this time moving along the broad belly of Earth Mother, searching for safety, searching for sustenance.

But these thoughts are for tomorrow. Today is the slow ripple of grass in the wind, the smooth rolling motion of mother's movement about the savannah, the steady drum of her heart, each beat a promise; "You're safe, You're safe, You're safe..."

Soon enough she will leave the pouch to face the world's dangers alone, but today she rests in mother's cool shadow. Today she is safe.

Few animals have developed a better system of insuring that their young are well cared for. Of all the nests, dens, burrows and other shelters in which young animals spend their first weeks and months, none can compare with Kangaroo's pouch in providing the vital mother/child link that is the great comfort of infancy and youth. Kangaroo need only to look at her belly to make sure her young are safe, enveloped in her warm, protective presence. Invoke mother Kangaroo for her maternal medicine powers when you need the confidence and stability that comes from a feeling of security and safety.

The kangaroo leaves the womb while still an undeveloped embryo and climbs through the fur of its mother's belly to her pouch, where it will spend about two months before it is ready to leave from time to time in search of food. The embryo is entirely without protection during this all-important trip, lacking even limbs with which to climb, pulling itself along with the tiny buds that will someday be legs. Yet every kangaroo living is a testament that this unlikely journey can be made. Invoke Kangaroo for help in caring for yourself when you feel most vulnerable. Call on this tiniest of kangaroos for the instinct to protect and nurture your inner child.

Leopard

Night has come to the jungle. The moon drops a thin light through the leafy canopy, but her pale efforts are swallowed by the deep shadows that shroud the forest floor. Through the thick darkness Leopard walks, alone, alert. The night holds no secrets for Leopard, the shadows conceal no surprises. They are her allies as she waits for that sudden rustle, the careless, too quick burst of activity that means a prey has been found, a meal is at hand.

For months now, these startled flurries of frightened movement have come less and less for Leopard. Drought has parched throats and shrunk bellies throughout the jungle, thinned the herds on the savannah, lit new and desperate fires in thousands of wild, hungry eyes. Many cats have left, searching for more promising watering holes, but Leopard has remained, the ruthless but realistic hunter, satisfied with a mouse if a deer is not to be found. No false pride for Leopard, no disdaining the modest gain. Survival is a series of small steps. And so Leopard walks the dry night, waiting for the sudden rustle, waiting for the soothing rain.

Of all the large cats, Leopard is the one most able to adapt herself to changing conditions. She varies her hunting methods and food sources depending on the situation at hand. This means that Leopard can live in many diverse climates and terrains. Because of this, Leopard is the most widely distributed of all the cats, roaming throughout the African continent and finding homes from Turkey to China,

The Way of the Animal Spirits

from Siberia to the East Indies. Invoke Leopard medicine for help in handling unexpected changes. Leopard teaches us to harmonize with our environment, making suitable changes so that we may thrive.

Leopard adapts not only to her environment, but to those with whom she shares that environment. Thanks to her furtive style of hunting that combines concealment, speed and timing, Leopard can catch many different species of small, elusive animals. Because of this, she doesn't have to compete with Lion or Tiger, who hunt much bigger game. Leopard teaches us that we don't have to win spectacular victories to be successful. Leopard says, "Behind a successful life is a long series of small and steady gains."

Leopard hunts alone and at night. We invoke Leopard for the ability to understand the mysteries of the darkness, the subconscious, the shadow aspect of our innermost selves. We can invoke Leopard medicine for assistance in developing occult powers and psychic sensibilities, and when delving into the magical arts or attempting to make the subconscious more accessible to the conscious mind. Leopard teaches us to face darkness and the shadow side of ourselves and the universe with courage, dignity and grace. She helps us to embrace all aspects of life — the sorrow and the joy, the darkness and the light.

Some Leopards have given up their spots, which provide such excellent camouflage for resting by day in the dappled light of trees, to wear the jet-black hues of night. These leopards are called panthers, and are even more efficacious when dealing with life's shadow side than their spotted cousins.

Lion

When one reflects on the multitude of animal beings Earth Mother has created, one is struck by how She often takes flesh and feather, fur and claw, and somehow fashions this rough clay around an idea so that an animal is the essence of that principle — a living, breathing symbol of a virtue or an ideal. How else can we explain the universal recognition of Eagle's nobility and Bull's dangerous strength. What accounts for our innate attraction to Dog's furry love or the intuitive respect for Snake's fanged stare?

Lion is one of those creatures who embody a certain attribute, and the characteristic that we find at the very core of Lion, that flows through that lithe body like blood through the veins, is elegance — unadorned, undeniable elegance. Whether bounding across the open plain in pursuit of a fleeing antelope or playfully cuffing a rambunctious cub, Lion moves, Lion lives, with an inner grace that is the birthright of royalty. No wonder he has been christened the King of Beasts.

When we consider the role of Lion in shamanic work, we should examine both the male and female lion, for each has certain medicine powers to teach and knowledge to share. Of course, it is fine to invoke them both; in shamanism, as in nature, their abilities complement each other.

Lion has long been associated with the Sun God. The male's flowing mane is likened to the rays emanating from the Sun, and the yellow coloring of Lion recalls the sun's bright hue. In ancient Egypt, the prowess and great-

78

ness of the female lion was recognized and honored, and she was worshiped as Sekhmet, the Sun Goddess, a powerful and fierce lioness diety.

As the largest of all the cat clans, female lion is the mightiest hunter. In size, strength and sheer power, she is without equal among her peers. The gifts of Lioness are many. That is why many tribal peoples invoke her medicine powers for strength, vitality, health, energy, prosperity and good luck.

Lion is the only one of the big cats who regularly hunts animals larger than herself. Therefore, we invoke Lion medicine when we undertake any large and difficult task. Her medicine can instill us with the courage, the power and the daring to pull it off.

Lioness, with her sharp claws and teeth, has been well equipped by nature for survival. But more important to her success as a hunter than these physical advantages is her abilty to cooperate with other lions. Unable to outrun her quarry, a lioness will join with the other female members of her pride in finding and bringing down an otherwise unapproachable animal.

Finding a suitable prey, the lions will sneak up on their victim, fanning out in a semi-circle to prevent an escape. It may take hours to get close enough to attempt a kill, slowly moving forward, waiting crouched in deep grasses or behind a clump of bushes till they can creep a bit closer. If the lions are spotted before thay are in a position to make their move, the prey makes its escape and the pride goes hungry. Therefore, Lion must exercise great patience, intelligence and cooperation to get close enough to spring a surprise attack. Call upon Lion to invoke these qualities into yourself.

Lion is a very adaptable hunter, adopting strategies to compensate for her weaknesses. Invoke Lion when you need to use your strengths and your wit to overcome your limitations.

While the female lions do most of the hunting, it is the job of the male lions to defend the territory, which they do by patrolling the area and roaring ferociously at all invaders. Lion teaches us to roar when necessary, to stay aware of our rights and to fearlessly assert ourselves when those rights are threatened.

When Lion is on the open plains where there isn't much cover, she will hunt at night. In areas where there is more cover, she will also hunt by day. Lion walks with assurance in the darkness of night and in the light of day. Therefore, we can invoke Lion medicine for balance between the heart and the mind, between the emotions and the intellect, between the conscious and the subconscious mind. Lion accepts and understands the energies of light and darkness, and walks with confidence in either realm.

Lizard

Lizard medicine is about survival and transformation. He is a living symbol of the vanished days of prehuman history — times of tar pits and dinosaurs.

Lizard was old before humankind appeared on the planet. He was created in and for another world, where mammalian instincts like the need to touch, communicate and love didn't exist. Not for Lizard the warm jumble of a Meercat pile or Monkey's instinctive grooming of his peers. Lizard's needs and motivations are much simpler — to find food, to mate, to avoid danger, to survive — and survive he has. While countless other reptiles have gone into extinction, Lizard still can be found in many areas of the world.

Perhaps we look down on Lizard as less than ourselves because of what we perceive as his limited outlook, but we would do better to honor him as our elder, a reptilian ancestor who lives on at the core of our somewhat expanded brain. When we feel the need to flee or to fight, that is Lizard sending his commands — basic, primal, but as useful now as during the time of the brontosaurus. Invoke Lizard to get in touch with that part of yourself concerned with survival.

Yet, even as Lizard teaches us about survival and the past, he points the way to a glorious future, to the unlimited potential for transformation which is inside us all and to the undreamed of possibilities which await us. Lizard is the father of the Bird Clan, for all birds evolved from lizards. When we see Lizard sunning himself on a rock, rough skinned, earthbound, fast but not particularly graceful, we

81

rarely stop to consider that Lizard is the clay from which Earth Mother fashioned such creatures as Eagle, Hawk, Sparrow and Swan. Somehow Lizard changed his scales into feathers and took to the air, achieving a transcendence and freedom which we humans have struggled to attain for eons. In fact, some Lizards seem to be taking to the air before our very eyes. In Asia and Indonesia can be found the flying dragon or flying lizard, a tree dweller who is equipped with wing-like folds of skin that act as a parachute to soften landings when leaping from tree to tree.

Invoke Lizard medicine in your personal quest for transformation, especially during the discouraging times when the path seems so long and difficult and the goal seems so far away. Recall Lizard's long crawl through the dust to the air, and know that you can truly reach any height to which you aspire.

Some lizards such as Gecko have the ability to break off their own tail by a spontaneous muscle contraction and then regenerate a new one. Often in our evolution there comes a time when we have to give up a part of ourselves, especially our preconceptions about reality, our ideas, in order to reach a new level of understanding. This can be difficult and painful, but when we let go of old ways of thinking, new notions form and develop that increase our understanding and awareness. We invoke Lizard medicine for the courage to let go of the old and the energy to create something new and better.

Lynx

We know less about this mysterious cat than we do about the larger cats, for Lynx is perhaps the most elusive and secretive of all the felines. She lives in wilderness areas of Canada, Alaska and the northernmost regions of the United States, and subsists mainly on Snowshoe Hare.

Lynx is the Medicine Keeper of the ancient mysteries and deep subconscious secrets. Her medicine wisdom concerns occult wisdom, positive magic and the wise use of power. Invoke Lynx (and feel honored if she comes) for developing great psychic powers and deep intuitive wisdom.

All cats are keepers of mystery powers (which is why they are so highly regarded in Egyptian and Tibetan monasteries), but Lynx is the most secretive keeper of the deepest mysteries. You should work with the medicine power of Lynx only when you feel grounded and well-balanced, for it is powerful medicine.

Lynx represents all that is fleeting, elusive, rare, hard to hold, yet beautiful. Lynx possesses a refined, subtle energy — always alert, always aware. By invoking Lynx, we may discern the sublte shades and implications of a situation and see through the secret deceptions of others.

Lynx knows the value of silence. She knows that silence holds many secrets that we fail to comprehend because we spend so much time bombarded by various types of noise — talk, television, stereos, traffic, etc. Lynx is the keeper of silence. Invoke her if you seek a quiet life in a quiet atmosphere.

Meercat

It is sunrise in the Kalahari desert and the Meercat clan slowly awakens. All sleep together in a Meercat pile. Here and there a sleepy movement can be seen in the jumble of furry bodies cozily intertwined in their communal burrow. As eyes open one by one to the light of the new day, the constant loving interaction which is the hallmark of life in a Meercat clan begins. Meercat is the only social animal on earth with absolutely no authoritarian hierarchy. The strong groom the weak, the old look after the young and all live in peace and unity.

Soon the clan leaves the burrow to go out and forage for food. While out foraging, the older meercats give any youngster pointers on where to find the choicest pickings. The elders teach all the young, and the young learn from all the elders, not just their parents.

At noon, the clan seeks cool shade in which to rest. There they will sit out the heat of the day while one meercat stands guard, ever alert to predators. If a dangerous snake enters their territory, they band together to drive it away. By evening, the meercats are back in their burrow, grooming, touching and interacting with utter harmony and love.

Meercat medicine teaches us to live socially, yet without the negative attributes of hierarchy. We invoke Meercat for the ability to live in harmony and equality with each other. Those who feel isolated and lonely can invoke Meercat to help manifest a loving community of friends. Let Meercat lead you to your clan.

85

Moose

He is heard before he is seen, his bellowing call fracturing the tranquility of the deep woods, silencing the small sounds that moments before had echoed through the forest. Soon the underbrush announces his approach. The tops of saplings quiver as eighteen hundred pounds of muscle brush them aside, and fallen branches crackle as broad hooves crush them into the earth.

Another trumpet-throated blast and he moves into the clearing. Though the brown coat is coarse, the huge nose is soft as velvet and under the throat hangs a wispy beard. But the most striking thing about this magnificent creature are the antlers, spanning over six feet from tip to tip, that rest atop the huge head like a sprawling crown.

He is a member of the Deer Clan, but nothing about Moose suggests the timidity of his lithe cousins as he walks serenely through the thick forests of the northern United States and Canada. Moose is noted for the strict and punctual feeding schedule that he maintains, and for the uncannily precise way in which he regulates his nutritional intake in a harsh environment. When scientists study his decision making process they find that Moose always makes the most energy efficient choices no matter what the constraints of his environment. In this way, Moose is like the manager of a business who must coordinate all the variables so that the business thrives. Invoke Moose to enhance organizational skills and managerial abilities. Call on him for help in setting priorities.

The Way of the Animal Spirits

Moose is well known for his loud and hearty bellow, proclaiming his pride and his love of life, and as the largest of the Deer Clan, Moose is associated with power, confidence, self-esteem, strength and potency. Moose medicine is valued for its ability to empower, yet as Moose's spirit infuses us with power, Moose also shows us how to use that power in a sane, organized, life-affirming way. This is a most helpful medicine to invoke when pursuing a career, for his energy is efficient and success-oriented. Moose teaches us how to put our power and our energy to practical use while not losing sight of the bigger picture.

Mountain Lion

Mountain Lion is one of the largest and most poweful of the cats in North America. She posesses all the shared medicine powers of the cat clan — the grace, the mystery, the otherworldliness.

A number of American Indian tribes held Mountain Lion in high regard. Mountain Lion is a loner — seldom seen and silent — able to eke out a living in the fiercest of environments. She will travel long distances for food and can have a vast hunting area, especially in the desert.

Once Mountain Lion roamed all over the Americas, but farmers and hunters have gradually confined her to more or less protected areas such as national parks and reserves. Mountain Lion usually does her best to avoid contact with humans but, because we are everywhere encroaching on the wilderness she needs to sustain herself, she has lately begun to enter the towns. Southern California newscasts regularly air stories of another Mountain Lion spotted in the suburbs. Now that she can retreat no further from civilization, now that there is too little land to hunt, Mountain Lion is coming to us — for food, for water, for help. She reminds us of our responsibility to herself and the countless other varieties of life found on Earth Mother that are endangered by humankind.

Invoke Mountain Lion for the ability to remain silent and the courage to walk alone. We also invoke Mountain Lion for grace, an understanding of the mysteries and the ability to survive in the harshest environments.

Mouse

Over 25% of all the animals who dwell upon Earth Mother are members of the Mouse clan. Mouse may be small, but she is extremely successful, perhaps the most prolific and varied of all the mammals.

In the course of history, whenever a new habitat, a new opportunity or a new challenge came along, Mouse met it by adapting and diversifying. For example, there are aquatic mice with webbed feet who eat fish, burrowing mice with sharp, powerful claws and desert mice who can go a long time without water. Grasshopper Mouse eats insects and Mole Mouse spends most of her life underground. Mouse bestows wildly successful adaptability on all who invoke her.

Perhaps Mouse's most valuable medicine is her awareness of the small and subtle things in life. She lives close to the earth and notices things as she forages for the food that larger animals overlook. Invoke Mouse for an appreciation of the little things in life.

Tiny, unconquerable Mouse shows us by her great success that although something or someone seems small and unimportant, it may still possess great wisdom and power.

Mouse says, "Look close, look closer. Feel with your whiskers, feel with your nose. Get right down into life and appreciate the little joys, the small wonders, that life has to offer."

Opossum

High above the forest floor, Opossum hangs by his strong, rope-like tail from the uppermost branch of a pine tree. Few beings view the world as Opossum is seeing it now, suspended upside down between heaven and earth, the sky at his feet, the green earth circling around his shoulders. His sharp eyes and ears pick out the sights and sounds of the forest, but he makes no effort to enter the teeming world below. Opossum is a loner, keeping to himself most of the time, avoiding trouble whenever possible. He simply listens, looks and waits, contemplating the world from this wide, weird perspective, and in so doing, seeing what others might miss. This is his life and, for Opossum, this is enough.

Opossum is unique among the mammals of North America. He is the continent's only marsupial, whose young, like the infant kangaroo, crawl through the mother's fur to spend its last months of development in her pouch. But the most unusual trait of Opossum is his tendency to hang suspended by his tail. The world Opossum sees at this time is not the same as that of his upright forest peers and therein lies his great medicine power — the ability to see things differently than others see them. Call upon Opossum when you feel the need to modify orthodox world views, society's or your own, to look at things in unusual and creative ways and, hopefully, to see a bit more than you have seen before.

Shamanic Wisdom II

Opossum is a loner, preferring his own company, keeping his own counsel. Solitude can be especially valuable to those just beginning to look at the world in new ways and needing time to evaluate what they have discovered, but many people are uncomfortable spending time with just themselves. Invoke Opossum medicine to teach you the joys of being alone. Ask him for guidance in using this sometimes difficult blessing.

When an enemy confronts Opossum, he often plays "dead." Opossum medicine wisdom teaches us to avoid violent confrontation through passive resistance whenever possible.

Opossum is an excellent climber, slowly reaching the topmost limbs of the tallest trees to reach flowers and nectar. That is why Opossum medicine is also about striving slowly and carefully to the pinnacle to reach fulfillment.

Opossum Speaks

I live my life in solitude,
To sense Earth Mother's every mood.
To be alone is my own choice.
It helps me hear that inner voice.
My eyes perceive a different view;
When upside down, the world looks new.

Otter

Because Otter doesn't have to try too hard to make a living, she has plenty of time on her hands that she puts to good use enjoying herself. Otter spends most of her time in the water, where her lithe body, short, sleek fur and flat tail made her an excellent swimmer. She quickly and effortlessly meets her food requirements with fish, eels, crayfish and other crustaceans, so she has plenty of time to relax and have fun. Invoke Otter medicine to become efficient in your work, so that you have lots of time to enjoy life.

This efficiency is the key to Otter's happiness. Her medicine wisdom teaches us to take care of the mundane things quickly and well, provide for ourselves easily, and then get in touch with the playful child within. For those who are too serious, invoke Otter for a more playful outlook on life.

Otter has many stiff, sensitive whiskers, not only on her snout but even on her elbows, to help her seek out food and judge the water's turbulence. Call upon Otter medicine for sensitivity and the ability to intuitively "feel" our way through life, and to intuit the emotional atmosphere of the people and situations we encounter.

Otter's affinity with water attunes her to the deep mysteries of this female element and acquaints her with water's flowing, receptive, emotional nature. Otter understands the role of female energies in creation and can lead us to the Goddess aspect of the Great Spirit, and also to the feminine within us, whether we are male or female.

93

Shamanic Wisdom II

Otter is very expressive and communicative. She communicates with chuckles, twitters, chirps, purrs, coos, growls and often says "Hah?" in an inquiring tone of voice. Invoke her spirit to make your words sparkle. With Otter in your mind and your heart, you can develop verbal expressiveness and eloquence.

Otter is one of the few members of the animal clans who use tools. Sea Otter will sometimes float on her back in the water and use a rock to crack open a shellfish resting on her chest. Call upon her for the energies of resourcefulness and inventiveness.

Otter is very inquisitive, always bursting with curiosity. Her energy inspires us to question and search for answers — to look into the great mysteries of the universe. But always remember the great fun Otter has making her investigations and be careful not to let your questions make you too serious. What good is knowledge without joy?

Invoke Otter for playfulness, joy, love of life, love of our bodies, laughter and happiness. Otter is the enlightened clown of the Animal Clan. Otter says, "You can learn in fear or in pain if you wish, but if you want to learn in laughter, I can teach you how."

Otter Invocation

Fill my life with joy and play,
Send me laughter every day.
Teach me to live happily.
Otter Spirits, live in me!

Owl

Humanity has been fascinated with Owl since at least the Old Stone Age, when figures of owls were carved on a cave wall in what would become southern France.

Owl was associated with the goddesses of many early civilizations. For example, Athene, the Greek goddess of wisdom, was often depicted with an owl on Her shoulder. We invoke Owl for wisdom as well as for deep intuitive knowing and the ability to discern hidden truths.

Owl is well-equipped for the life she leads. The Lakotah Indians called Owl "hush-wing" because the shape and texture of her wings allow her to fly silently through the night in search of prey. Owl has excellent eyes set in a head that can turn almost completely around. When Owl locates prey, she quickly swoops down unheard and captures it with her sharp talons. Owl moves well in the world for which she was made. Invoke Owl medicine when moving through those dark, uncertain times when much seems to be unclear or unknown. Invoke her aid in seeing the obstacles and opportunities and in matching your skills and talents with the demands of a situation.

Because Owl is of the night, of the mystery, she has often been feared by cultures unable to accept the dark side of reality. But she has also been invoked as a benevolent and powerful ally. The Romans used an owl symbol as an amulet against the Evil Eye. The ancient Chinese used owl ornaments to protect their homes from fire and the Japanese nailed figurines of owls to their houses in times of famine.

Shamanic Wisdom II

Indian mothers used pillows of owl feathers to lull a restless child to sleep. And in Israel gray owls near the crops were considered a good omen.

Owl has often been linked with the moon, such as in the Indian myth of the *War of the Owls and Crows* which symbolized the conflict between the moon and the sun. Owl's struggle against Crow was so that humanity would acknowledge that there is a hidden world in all of us that needs to be explored, a world best glimpsed in the moonlight. Invoke Owl when you feel the need to explore the subtle spaces of reality, or the subconscious. Owl teaches us to discern the truth and face what we find.

Owl is sacred to many versions of the Triple Goddess of the Moon, such as Lilith and Anath. Even owl eggs, white and almost round, betoken an affinity with moon. The Moon Goddess and Her Owl companion grant magical powers to those who honor them.

An ally of witches and those who work magic, Owl is much prized as a hush-wing of occult and hidden powers. Owl brings a knowledge of the night, the wisdom of the shadows. She teaches psychic powers, magic and occult abilities, and awakens us to the Moonlight Vision.

Owl Invocation

Feather of silence, eye with a hood,
I will reclaim the night's power for good,
Through shadow and blackness, that I might see;
Owl Spirit, live in me!

Peacock

Wild Peacock makes his home in northern Asia's forests and jungles, where he has long been admired by the societies in that region for his magnificent plumage. Hindus associate Peacock with Indra, the god of war, rain and thunder. Peacock merits this sacred status for his courageous spirit and the ferocity with which he will attack snakes, as well as his habit of calling loudly and dancing joyfully whenever there is a sign of rain.

Because Peacock can defend people from snakes, he is commonly thought of as a guardian bird granting general protection. He is especially valued for providing psychic protection. Folk wisdom holds that keeping a peacock feather in the home helps to safeguard the energy in that environment.

Peacock's exuberant dance reminds us that when we move rythmically and with joy, we acknowledge our bodies and revere our inherent sensuality. Expression through dance honors the world of incarnate sensation and recognizes the cosmic dance in which we join, in ecstasy and with a rejoicing that our bodies can't contain, but which flows from our heart to our muscles in spontaneous movement. This type of expression can be thought of as a moving prayer, an impulsive celebration of life.

Indian folklore informs us that seeing a peacock is an auspicious sign of good luck and serenity. Many people invoke Peacock for peace of mind, relaxation, protection, rain and the ability to joyously express oneself.

Penguin

For weeks, the biting winds of the Antarctic winter have raged around Penguin, pelting him with stinging bullets of ice and bringing endless blankets of cold, wet snow. If he were alone the bitter cold might have killed him long ago, and for one isolated and friendless in this vast, white landscape, perhaps such a fate would be almost merciful. But whatever deprivations Penguin must suffer in his spare, polar home, lack of companionship is not one of them.

Penguin belongs to a colony of thousands of penguins, and huddled together against the elements, sharing the warmth of their bodies, they are able to endure conditions in the most inhospitable region on the planet. Penguin has endured because he has adapted. Indeed, few creatures have had to adapt more in order to overcome the challenges of their environment.

Technically, Penguin is a bird, though he has forsaken the sky for the icy waters and snow-covered coasts of his Antarctic home where he feeds on fish, squid and crustaceans. He has evolved his wings into flippers and developed webbed toes. Penguin has so fitted his body to the water that he can swim as well as Sea Lion.

While molding the contours of his body to the demands of his environment, Penguin also tailored his social practices to those requirements. Because the Antarctic offered so few materials for building shelter and no other options as far as protection from the elements, the penguin colony became its own shelter, each black and white body a warm brick in a loose, waddling wall of Penguin flesh, ever shifting and full of drafts but nevertheless keeping the worst of the cruel weather at bay.

Penguin's parenting practices, too, reflect the paucity of resources in his environment; the webbed feet of the parents serve as a nest for their single egg. A penguin couple take turns holding the egg on their feet, covered by a fold of their abdomen, through the entire incubation period so that it is kept safely off the polar ice.

We invoke Penguin medicine when we must change and adapt to meet new situations in our own lives, no matter how radical these changes may be, for surely no one has shown more ability at effective change than Penguin.

Penguin is a very social animal who lives in huge colonies, yet is also strictly monogamous. This is a rare combination in nature and serves to show us an alternative to what might be called the "Best Friend Syndrome" — that type of relationship where a couple become involved with each other to the exclusion of the rest of the world. Often they start relying on each other for everything, and everything is just too much to expect from one person. The relationship may eventually collapse under the strain of its own weight.

Penguin medicine wisdom teaches us how to enrich our lives through satisfying interaction with a wide variety of people while keeping our primary commitment strong and secure.

Porcupine

In a world of tooth and claw, Porcupine has chosen a unique way to defend herself. She simply uses the strong, sharp quills which cover much of her body to prick any animal who threatens her. This method is unorthodox but effective, since Porcupine is one of the few animals on earth who does not seem to be threatened by extinction. Porcupine's medicine teaches us how to use the unusual abilities we have been given. Some of these gifts may seem a bit odd, they may seem useless at times, but if we explore them fully instead of wondering why we are not like everyone else, we will truly live a full and satisfying life.

Perhaps, when the blessings of the universe were distributed, Porcupine complained about her quills and asked to be given sharp claws and teeth like other animals. Sadly, many of these animals are dwindling in numbers while Porcupine prospers. Maybe you've wondered why you have been drawn to walk a path of shamanism and spirituality in this mundane society, why you couldn't be satisfied with a life of consumerism and career like everyone else. Porcupine medicine wisdom reminds us to treasure our uniqueness, to treasure our "otherness" as a powerful tool in our spiritual survival.

Porcupine is a peaceful being at heart, never looking for a fight. If a potential enemy crosses her path, she prefers to work things out nonviolently. When threatened, she will often shake her tail, rattle her quills and stamp her feet as a warning signal. However, if her warnings are not heeded,

The Way of the Animal Spirits

Porcupine will not sit passively and wait for trouble to come to her. She will turn around and run sideways or backwards into her enemy. When her quills penetrate her enemy's skin they detach from her body. Porcupine medicine wisdom teaches us to do whatever we can to keep tense situations from escalating and to give fair warning when we feel threatened.

Porcupine is an excellent climber who often climbs trees to great heights to reach the best food. Porcupine is intelligent and has a very good memory. The young are born with their eyes open and can climb trees and defend themselves just a few days after birth. Porcupine is invoked for the inspiration to reach the heights, good memory and the ability to express oneself and stand up for oneself in unique ways.

Prairie Dog

Prairie Dog, a member of the squirrel clan, lives in large towns with underground networks of tunnels and burrows that might extend as much as 160 square miles. So Prairie Dog medicine can be called upon by those of us who have to deal with the pressures of living in large urban communities.

No matter how extensive a Prairie Dog town is, when Prairie Dogs meet they will touch noses before passing. Prairie Dog medicine wisdom reminds us that in crowded urban situations, when it is so easy to look on all the other people as faceless bodies, we need to realize that each one of those bodies holds a special individual spirit, a human clan sibling who deserves to be noticed and acknowledged.

Prairie Dog relies heavily on his burrow for safety. He surrounds the entrance way to his burrow with mounded earth to keep it from flooding. Prairie Dog medicine wisdom teaches us to guard against being inundated by the deluge of pressures from the outside world.

Both sexes of the Prairie Dog play with the young and teach them the clan wisdom. Our society is witnessing the rapid evolution of traditional parenting responsibilities. The old roles are changing. Therefore, we invoke Prairie Dog to help us break the old stereotypes of parenting so that we can begin co-parenting our young.

Prairie Dog medicine is invoked for a sense of community, for valuing friends and companions.

Rabbit & Hare

Shy and alert, fleet of foot and ready to run rather than fight, Rabbit's medicine is a powerful one. She has even made her way into the dry consciousness of our own culture. We share a common idea about Rabbit's procreative powers, and we are not the first to notice this. Many cultures believed Rabbit grants fertility and honored her at the ancient European spring rebirth festival of Eostar. Our culture's dim memory of this is the Easter Bunny.

Rabbit and Hare rely on their ability to move quickly and to be ever alert to danger. The large ears detect the smallest sounds and large eyes enhance night vision. Rabbit is adapted to life in burrows, while Hare's adaptations allow for speeds up to fifty miles an hour. People mistakenly think that, because Rabbit and Hare run away from danger, they are cowardly. Perhaps it is more helpful to honor each animal's unique medicine powers. In this way we honor Earth Mother who created us all. When we judge a quality of an animal as a weakness we find, if we look deeper, that it is actually a wise gift given by Earth Mother, who wants all of her children to thrive and flourish. Rabbit and Hare do what they must to survive within the limitations and medicine gifts Earth Mother has given them, and they survive quite successfully.

Rabbit and Hare medicine teaches that some caution is wise in certain circumstances. Invoke Hare and Rabbit for alertness, attentiveness, awareness, fertility, creativity and renewal.

DIANE VERSTEEG 1983

Racoon

With her black bandit's mask and her tail ringed with convict stripes, Racoon resembles the forest's version of a petty thief. Even her habits fit this metaphor. Racoon is one of the most nocturnal of the animals, a true denizen of the night. And in addition to the foods she finds in nature, she's not at all adverse to raiding garbage cans and campsites for something to eat.

But Racoon is a likable being whose medicine powers include an appreciation of impish, humorous and playful energy. Racoon can be a wise and helpful guardian of people with these playful attributes. Racoon medicine wisdom shows us how to find the fun in life and helps us to see life's humor and paradox.

Well known for her curiosity, Racoon is invoked for the ability to fully scrutinize a situation or a subject. Racoon medicine is about constantly seeking, searching and staying interested in life.

Racoon's night time wanderings often take her to watery areas where she will feast on fish, frogs and other such fare. But Racoon is a very versatile hunter, settling for insects, fruit, rodents or earthworms.

Racoon's hands are capable of much more dextrous manipulation than most animals, useful for snatching a meal from the water as well as breaking into the "safest" of food containers pilfered from a campsite. For these reasons, Racoon is invoked for resourcefulness and versatility.

Raven & Crow

Sometime in the past, Raven and Crow built their nests in the dimly lit loft of humanity's subconscious; there they perch still. It is not difficult to understand how, seeing the black silhouettes in the sky, many diverse people recognize the shadow side of creation, flying out from time to time to remind us of what we've forgotten, of what we must still learn.

These two birds grant an understanding of the occult, of magic, of exploring new and different aspects of our own consciousness, which is the heart of magic. Their medicine power grants an acceptance of the mysteries and reminds us of the Native American Indian Prayer: "Thank you, Great Spirit, for the Mystery."

To many tribes of the North Pacific coast, Raven is an insatiable Trickster as well as a Transformer who manifested humanity from out of a clamshell and gifted us with fire and water. Many tribes invoke Raven for assistance in their healing ceremonies. Crow is also a Trickster figure to certain Plains tribes as well as guardian of the sacred laws. His knowledge of these mysteries enables Crow to bend reality, work magic, and travel astrally. Call upon Crow medicine for these medicine gifts, for his powers can help us transform and transcend the limitations of the body.

Crow is a survivor. Many of the animal Tricksters among the tribal peoples have been remarkable survivors during times of decrease and extinction for so many other animals. To make sure the offspring survive with less competition, Crow is the earliest breeder, mating in January, building a nest of twigs in February and laying eggs by March. With such a good start in life, no wonder Crow exudes confidence, asserting himself with pride and power.

Many peoples regard Raven and Crow as birds of prophecy. They are messengers to the higher powers, their strong wings fanning the smoke-wrapped prayers of the sacred pipe to the Great Spirit. Whenever you see Raven or Crow, send your prayer to them and ask them to carry your prayer to the Great Spirit. Raven is especially noted for his ability to manifest healing prayers and healing magic.

Raven loves to circle high among black storm clouds, and he is associated with storms, thunder and rain making magic.

The witches, druids and magicians of Northern Europe invoked them to increase magical powers and to add power to magical spells.

Welsh folklore tells us that those who honor Raven regain their sight — both physically and spiritually. The Irish speak of a certain kind of omniscience, of psychicly knowing and seeing all as "Raven's Knowledge." We invoke Raven for the gifts of prophecy and second sight.

The Welsh consider Raven and Crow to be truthful birds. This would seem to contradict the Indian's view of Raven and Crow until we remember that the Trickster is also the Transformer, blessing us by constantly changing reality. His mischievous, trickster side reminds us of the ironies and paradoxes inherent in Creation. His is a higher truth that embraces the mystery and the magic of Creation.

Rhinoceros

They meet at the border of their respective territo-ries, facing each other across a dusty no-man's land. Two male rhinoceroses stand motionless, menacing, seemingly ready to fight. The sharp horns of their snouts curve upwards like drawn swords; the small eyes set in the squat, gray bodies portend danger, like archers glimpsed through the tiny windows of a fortress.

There is to be no battle today, but a ritual that is actually a peace-keeping ceremony, allowing each warrior to assert his territorial claim and retain his dignity without bloodshed. First, the two rhinos will stand horn to horn and stare at each other. Then they will break away and whack their horns to the ground. This is repeated over and over until the ritual is finished and each one returns to his own territory.

Rhinoceros bestows the medicine wisdom of ritual and ceremony and reminds us how important these are for bringing ourselves into harmony. Some of us resonate to the traditional rituals our religion offers, while others look to the ancient ceremonies of the tribal peoples. Still others create their own ceremonies that have meaning and beauty to them. Rhinoceros medicine wisdom teaches us to regu-larly celebrate our sacred connection with spirit through ritual and ceremony.

A small bird called Oxpecker often accompanies Rhinoceros, hitching a ride on his massive back. Oxpecker eats insects and parasites who hide in the wrinkles and folds of Rhino's skin. Rhino's medicine includes the art of forming alliances and mutually beneficial relationships. He shows us how to communicate and coexist with species far different from our own.

Rhino loves water and derives much satisfaction from sitting, wallowing and rolling about in a muddy pond or river. Not only does he enjoy the cooling properities of the water, but the cooling mud that clings to his skin offers protection from biting flies. Let Rhino medicine wisdom inspire you to luxuriate, bask, delight, relish, enjoy and take deep satisfaction in all the natural, healthy pleasures that life has to offer.

As one of the longer lived animals, Rhino medicine is thought to bring longevity and health to those who honor and invoke him.

Rhinoceros Speaks

Sharp-tusked warrior, armored in mud —
My ritual skirmish is fought without blood.
My dignity's honored, but no life is lost.
The wars of the Rhino are fought without cost.
If only those people concerned with defense
Could organize battles that made so much sense.
They'd lay down their weapons — the sword and the lance,
And war would become a ritual dance.

Salmon

Salmon has long been honored as a fish of both deep wisdom and great mystery. Irish folklore attributes the gifts of prophecy and clairvoyance to Salmon, and Celtic folk wisdom informs us that Salmon medicine also grants to those who invoke her the power of telepathic prescience.

Salmon hatches in a river and then makes her way to the sea, only to return later in life to spawn in her home waters. The trip up the river is a dangerous and arduous trek. Salmon must have a great deal of endurance and determination to complete the journey.

We, too, often reach a place in our lives when we must return to our roots. Perhaps this is a return to the vicinity or values of our youth after a time of exploration in the wider world. Or perhaps our path looks back to a time and place older and farther away than our own past, back into the mists and mysteries of our species, our planet, our universe, to the ultimate answers for which we all search. Whatever our goal, in pursuing it we are searching for something that will make our lives whole. Creation is a cycle. The path we walk is circular, and each step we take brings us a bit closer to completion — of the circle and of ourselves.

Call upon Salmon's medicine power for the strength and stamina needed on your own journey of return, and for the wisdom to understand the mysteries that await your arrival.

Skunk

Skunk walks the night paths of the forest, moving slowly and confidently, taking her own sweet time foraging for delicacies in the underbrush. She is a small animal and does not appear to have any natural weapons that would warrant her relaxed attitude in a moonlit world filled with predators who are bigger, stronger, faster, sharper of claw and longer of tooth than herself. But Skunk has a secret weapon — two musk glands hidden at the base of her tail that can squirt a nauseating and foul-smelling liquid up to ten feet. Most other animal clans will go out of their way to avoid Skunk. They show great courtesy and deference toward her, so Skunk can go about her business at her own pace, knowing full well that the world will make way for her.

Unlike some other mammals whose method of defense is either lethal or injurious, Skunk protects herself in a way that does not cause any permanent injury and yet is one of the most effective defenses in the animal world. Skunk medicine teaches us to be assertive in creative ways that are effective but not destructive.

Most skunks warn their victims before they spray by stamping their front feet, walking with a stiff-legged gait and raising their tails. Skunk teaches us to be assertive and stand up for ourselves, and that asserting our rights will often avoid a confrontation. Reputation, respect and deference are the medicine powers that Skunk shares with us. She teaches us to develop those attributes for ourselves, and encourages us to offer these gifts to others. So much needless confrontation could be avoided if we would all accord each other the basic respect and dignity which is our right. Skunk knows that disrespect often causes a "psychic stink."

But Skunk knows that, at this point in our evolution, respect isn't freely given but must be earned, must be demanded, and that the best way to start getting respect is to demand it of yourself. Skunk teaches us to honor ourselves and to grow in self-esteem. He makes us realize that it is our demeanor and attitude that attracts or repels those with whom we come into contact. Skunk teaches those who are too meek and retiring to be assertive, and maybe put up just a little bit of a stink to build a reputation that will cause others to respect us and think twice before mistreating us.

The other animals must have laughed at Skunk on that creation morning when she chose musk glands and foul smell as her weapons. How they must have chuckled into their newly-clawed paws as she ambled off with her weird arsenal. But Skunk believed in herself and her unusual abilities, as she exhorts us to believe in ourselves and to develop our own unique powers. These powers might not seem, at first glance, to deserve respect, as they might not be seen by the mainstream culture as important. But if we honor them we will exude a strong aura of self-respect that others will respond to. Skunk says, "Don't let society's notions of what is best and noblest overly influence you. You are most empowered when you are empowered in your own, totally individual way."

Snake

Snake's forked tongue hisses truth to those who will hear, but Snake's medicine gifts are only for those who know how to receive her knowledge. For thousands of years our culture has viewed Snake with fear, wary of her power to inflict death and instinctively troubled by the reptilian wisdom hidden behind hooded eyes.

But why do we fear Snake? She is not intrinsically hideous to look at; no one can deny her elegant beauty. She is no more threatening than many animals who evoke a much less visceral response. We fear Snake because she forces us to confront issues our culture chooses to deny.

Snake has long been linked with the Goddess aspect of the Great Spirit. This is one reason why, in our patriarchal culture, which degrades the female aspect, Snake is seen as evil. Snake is also associated with death and rebirth through the many ancient serpent goddesses who symbolize the endless mystery of death and rebirth.

Snake is also seen as symbolic of phallic energy and has been linked throughout history with sexuality and sensuality. Snake says, "Enjoy earthly pleasure. Bask in the sun and relish sensuality and the gifts of the senses, for our sacred Earth Mother has bestowed these gifts on us all."

Many people the world over honor Snake as a teacher of all things magical, mystical, secret and psychic, and invoke Snake for occult abilities, an understanding of magic, transformation and ancient wisdom.

Shamanic Wisdom II

Snake can shed her skin and emerge renewed. For this reason, her medicine is invoked for renewal, longevity, rebirth, creativity and immortality. Because of Snake's ability to shed the old and grow into the new, we invoke Snake for the ability to transcend current limitations and go beyond restrictive beliefs and mindsets, as well as the ability to face change, transformation and metamorphosis.

In many cultures, Snake is often seen as a protective spirit. Folk wisdom from around the world attributes healing powers, protection and good fortune to Snake. Most North American Indians honor Snake; the Hopi honor Snake's medicine powers to bring rain to their arid lands.

Snake is associated with rainbows as well as rain. Australian indigenous peoples hold the Rainbow Snake in high regard as creator and bringer of fertility.

Snake scares us and intrigues us because she embodies, literally, the wisdom of the circle — no other being can form itself into a circle as she can. No other being can impart as clearly the lessons of the circle, or the medicine wheel, which symbolizes wholeness and completion. Snake shows us the eternal and mysterious turning of the medicine wheel of life, death and rebirth on a personal and cosmic level. She teaches us not to fear death, but to realize that Earth Mother in Her sacred wisdom has decreed continuous life, death and rebirth on a cellular and spiritual plane for all her children. Snake, holding her tail in her mouth, reminds us that life is a circle without end. She tells us that a full life embraces all aspects of the earth plane, and that a balanced life harmonizes with the cycles of nature.

Spider

Just as Spider, from her own body, spins intricate, ingenious and beautiful webs, so she can impart to those who invoke her the medicine gifts of creativity and imagination. Spider inspires us with a vision and gifts us with the manifestation power to weave our dreams into reality.

Most spiders weave their webs with silken thread in order to snare prey. Spiders who do not build webs hunt over the ground, but leave a safety line trailing behind them as they go. Spider is the fate-spinner, creating the conditions and the opportunity to get what she wants through careful and skillful preparation. But she also cautions us to have a safety line — options, security and alternate plans of action to fall back on when we begin new endeavors.

Female Spider builds a silken cocoon to cushion her eggs. Many eggs are laid, in some species a thousand at a time. When the baby spiders hatch they launch gossamer strands of silk into up-currents and so become airborne. In this way they all disperse to find a home of their own. Invoke Spider for independence and the courage to strike out on your own into the unknown, whether it be a physical, spiritual or emotional trip.

West Indian and West African tradition honors Anansi, a trickster spider of great cunning, and in some legends the Creator of the world.

Folklore informs us that "If you would live and you would thrive, let a spider run alive," and cautions against killing a spider lest you bring unneeded rain.

Squirrel

For millions of years the canopies of the earth's forests have been alive with the quick movements of Squirrel going about her many errands. She is one of the most industrious of Earth Mother's children, spending most of her time storing nuts or building a warm, sturdy, moss-lined nest in which to spend the winter. Squirrel's careful planning and persistence have allowed her to make a niche for herself on every continent on the planet except Australia, adjusting to virtually every terrain and living condition. Whether in lush tropical forests, the desert, the remote Canadian wilderness or the largest cities, Squirrel thrives. She is one of the most successful and numerous animals on earth, and her medicine gift of adaptability can be seen in the great diversity in the members of the Squirrel Clan. Call upon Squirrel medicine for success.

Squirrel has been worshipped for many centuries. The ancient Germanic peoples held the Red Squirrel to be sacred. Red Squirrel gives away her territory to her young, leaving her offspring a place to live and a way to eat, and truly these things are a precious legacy. We must also consider carefully what we will bequeath our children, spiritually as well as materially. Invoke the spirit of Red Squirrel to instill in us the wisdom to leave a legacy of place and sustenance for the next generation, to safeguard the global environment for the future.

Unlike Red Squirrel, Gray Squirrel shares her territory with the other adults. She does not compete with her

116

friends and relatives. She plays and mates and cuddles with her peers. Most of us who are too competitive and grasping can call upon Gray Squirrel medicine to loosen us up and to help us realize that if we can't enjoy life, we really have won nothing with all our competing.

From infancy, Squirrel buries nuts and seeds, intuitively preparing for winter. In harsh weather she will conserve her energy by hibernating, waking in the spring to consume the last of her stores. Squirrel inspires us to plan ahead and consider the future, always keeping a reserve of material and emotional resources.

Besides the ability to hibernate in winter when food is scarce, some members of the Squirrel clan can also sleep in summer during a drought when no food is available. They simply close off their den with grasses and go to sleep until the harsh conditions are over. Squirrel medicine encourages us to wait things out if life gets harsh, to go inward, to find a safe place to dream and meditate until conditions turn hospitable again, when spiritual and emotional nourishment are available.

Squirrel also teaches us that just as we plan, save, and hold on to some of our resources and energies to get us through the lean times, so we should give back to life as well. Squirrel always buries a few nuts and acorns that she will forget about; in this way she helps the forest to renew itself. Gray Squirrel helps Oak to multiply by burying acorns at a distance from the parent tree, and Douglas Pine Squirrel helps pine trees in the same way.

Swan

Dawn is breaking, and as the darkness fades, the first rays of the new sun find two pale silhouettes making their way across a pond. They move smoothly, silently, like ephemeral denizens of another world. They glide together on the water's mirror-still surface like elegant, unhurried ghosts, till the growing light reveals them to be, after all, beautiful but mundane members of our own reality — a swan couple, beginning yet another of many days together.

But perhaps there is something here that's not wholly of this world, or not nearly as much a part of it as we would hope. For there is a love between these two creatures, as deep as the night they're leaving and as pure as the down on their breasts, that bonds them to each other, intertwining their lives like the gently enmeshing ripples of their graceful passage.

This love expresses itself in a strict and loyal monogamy which will last until death, and in an affectionate, cooperative, satisfying partnership that could serve as a relationship model for almost any species, and especially our own.

Their courtship is a tender time, with the male caressing the female's neck while softly, gently calling to her. After mating, when there are eggs to be hatched, he will feed and guard her during the incubation period, and then he will assist her in protecting and feeding the baby swans (cygnets).

118

The Way of the Animal Spirits

When Swan's mate dies, she will go into a state of deep grieving. Sensitive humans can often tell by the sorrowful and mournful expression on Swan's face and by her stricken demeanor that she (or he) has lost a mate. Only after this period of deep mourning will Swan, if young enough, find another mate to commit to and love.

Our society lacks faith — in the Great Spirit, in each other, in ourselves. Yet the human soul is inspired, instructed and healed in a state of faith. Swan teaches us to commit to the people and the ideals we love — to cherish them, to guard and protect them, and to devote our lives to them — in perfect love and perfect trust. This kind of loyalty demands the courage to open up our heart to loss, and yet it awakens our spirit to true passion.

When we experience loss around the people and ideals we have committed to (and be assured that we will eventually experience loss, for everything dies, changes, undergoes transition — loss is a natural part of love and commitment), Swan medicine wisdom teaches us to mourn and grieve openly, to consciously acknowledge our loss so that the healing acceptance of transformation can begin. In this way, we learn to accept life, love and death — the great mystery dance of the universe.

Swan also gently helps us to move on after our grieving is done, richer and wiser from our experience, and find a new passion to which we can commit ourselves.

Swan's medicine gifts also include grace, beauty, psychic and intuitive powers, and the ability to move fluidly through alternative states of consciousness. Invoke Swan for all these powers.

Tiger

Tiger is the largest member of the cat clan. While there is only one species of tiger, there are many varieties whose markings and other characteristics vary widely depending on the local conditions. Siberian Tiger is the largest member of the clan.

Tiger is a solitary animal who hunts alone, usually during the evening and the early part of the night. Tiger prefers dense cover in order to conceal himself from his prey, but he will make use of whatever cover he finds. He prefers to hunt in tall, dry grasses. The golden color of the grasses blends with Tiger's body, and the black lines that accent his coat also break up the outline of his body as he stalks or lies motionless in ambush.

Since he must get fairly close to his prey if he is to have a chance at success, Tiger approaches very, very carefully, planning each paw placement with exquisite care, frequently pausing to examine the situation. He approaches at a crouch, making himself all but invisible, till he is as close as the cover will allow so that he can take his prey in a few swift bounds.

Tiger medicine wisdom teaches us to make good use of whatever opportunities and good breaks happen to come our way. Tiger shows us, by example, how to take our time and do things carefully, to pause from time to time and assess the situation. But Tiger also encourages us to act swiftly and with resolve when the time is right and the opportunity we have waited for finally presents itself.

Shamanic Wisdom II

Rather than passively waiting for an unsuspecting animal to cross his path, Tiger will usually go in active search of a meal. Only about once in every ten or so tries is Tiger successful at catching his prey, but this doesn't discourage him in the least. Many people invoke Tiger medicine for the inspiration of initiative and persistence. We call upon Tiger for the ability and the heart to find a worthy goal and to pursue that goal until we reach it, no matter how many times we may fail.

The only important social unit among tigers is the one between a mother and her young, because Tiger's hunting methods and environment usually don't allow for too much contact. Therefore, Tiger medicine is called upon by those of us who wish to manifest independence and self-sufficiency.

When Tigers do meet in the wilderness, they are friendly toward one another. Sometimes we find ourselves in a situation where the opportunities to meet new people are very limited. In these situations we can invoke Tiger medicine to help us appreciate and interact well with whomever is in our immediate environment, even if they're not our first choice of companions.

Tiger Invocation

Silent power, black and gold,
May my careful dreams unfold
Quietly, persistently.
Tiger Spirit, live in me!

Turtle & Tortoise

Tortoise has the longest lifespan of any animal on the earth. The Giant Tortoise has been known to live over 150 years. Her hard shell, leathery skin and patient, cautious nature afford excellent protection from any predators she may come across.

Many American Indians associate Turtle with Earth Mother. Turtle represents the female, or Goddess, aspect of the Great Spirit, because of the deep sense of stability, perseverance and endurance that one feels around Turtle.

Everyone knows the slow but steady pace that Tortoise uses to eventually get wherever she needs to go. Aesop even immortalized Tortoise and her plodding but effective methods in his fable about Tortoise's race with Hare. Hare was swifter, but Tortoise won. And that is why Tortoise is invoked by many people for the medicine powers of longevity, protection, wisdom, perseverance and ancient knowledge.

Sea Turtle buries many eggs in the sand at one time, then leaves them to be incubated by the sun. When the little turtles hatch they race eagerly to the sea, but most of them are eaten by seagulls before they can reach the safety of the waves. So many are born, however, that a few of the fastest and luckiest are assured of survival. That is why every Turtle that is alive has the great medicine power of good luck, good fortune and being in the right place at the right time. Invoke Turtle for these medicine gifts.

123

Weasel

Like the bejeweled sheath of a king's sword, the exquisite majesty of our planet conceals an ever present potential for war. A certain amount of fierceness is needed to survive on earth and Weasel, even though she usually weighs less than 4 1/2 pounds, is one of the planet's foremost warriors. She is a formidable hunter who uses cunning, stealth and her renowned fierceness to bring her prey down. Her ferociousness is of such an extraordinary degree that the ancients associated Weasel with Nemesis, the goddess of retribution.

Because Weasel is so tiny, her abilities are often underestimated. Weasel medicine wisdom teaches us how to look beyond the superficial, to never underestimate other people or situations. She helps us to size up things accurately no matter what the appearance.

Tiny Weasel is one of the most widespread carnivores in the world. She shows us that small size and few resources are not barriers to success, but that strength of will and tenacity of purpose can overcome obstacles.

Weasel does most of her hunting underground in deep snow. Therefore, her medicine powers include the ability to unearth the hidden, obscure, occult and mysterious. Weasel helps us to get in touch with our subconscious mind, our deep inner intuition, our real feelings and with the supernatural powers deep within ourselves.

Weasel medicine is invoked for determination, courage, cunning, fearlessness and tenacity.

124

The Way of the Animal Spirits

Weasel Speaks

I walk the world a warrior,
Survive by tooth and claw,
Fighting out my battles
By the forest's ancient law.

Don't be quick to judge me
By the merits of my size.
My strength lies in the fierceness
That smoulders in my eyes.

I grant to you the cunning
To overcome the odds.
I give to you the courage
That I won from the gods.

I show to you the secret
Of the fearless way I live.
The wisdom of the warrior
Is the gift I have to give.

Whale

Legend has it that long ago, before Lemuria was swallowed by the sea, Whale lived on the land. The rising tides that scattered humanity to the corners of the earth also forced Whale to seek refuge in the ocean. There Whale evolved from a creature of the land into a creature of water. Her body changed, adapted to its new surroundings, until she was more at home in the deep than in the world of sky and sunshine and wind.

Whale is a wise and powerful being who has been honored by many cultures. Ancient Arabians told of Bahamut, an enormous Whale whose huge body was the base upon which the world rested; earthquakes were caused by Bahamut's movements. Indians on the east coast of Central America revered Whale. They called her Mamacocha, or "Mother Sea." Whale was a totem of some of the Indian tribes of the North American Pacific coast, who believed that Whale could sink the canoes of their enemies. Among peoples who know the sea, whale's teeth have long been prized as badges of rank and potent amulets, imparting to their possessor some of Whale's tremendous physical power.

But we do not have to kill Whale or wear her teeth to share in her medicine powers. We need only invoke, honor and pray to Whale Spirits. Whale is one of the most intelligent animals on the planet. Powerful, ancient and wise, we invoke Whale for her great medicine gifts.

The ocean is the archive of Earth Mother, a vast, jumbled record of the numberless directions life has taken on this planet throughout the eons. Whale has spent uncountable ages learning the secrets of the sea. Whale's medicine power is a knowledge of the unseen past, the secret places of those things deep in the subconscious, reachable only through the murky waters of intuition. Invoke Whale medicine to help you explore our planet's hidden history as well as the bottomless spaces within yourself. She is a huge, warm presence to have nearby when navigating the mysterious depths — of the ocean or of our own mind.

Some Whales have teeth, while others have evolved comblike structures called baleen plates with which to strain seawater for tiny organisms such as krill. These plates let sand and other particles pass through but trap the nutritious krill. In this way, Whale takes only what she needs from the sea; she doesn't ingest those things which won't nourish her, or might even do her harm. Baleen Whale medicine teaches us to sample huge portions of the life around us, be it experience, or ideas, but to discard what we don't need, keeping only that which nourishes.

The song of Humpback Whale is beautifully haunting and complex. Whales in the same region all use the same song, yet add their own individualized flourishes. Whale teaches us to participate in the life of our society, sing the archetypal songs of our culture — its assumptions, beliefs, behaviors — and still maintain our own unique "style."

We invoke Whale for power, wisdom, intelligence, discriminating ability, intuitive knowing and the ability to sing your own song and express your own individuality.

D.S.VERSTEEG © 19

Wolf

He haunts the empty stretches of forest and plain, a lean silhouette glimpsed on a distant ridge, a lonely howl piercing the moonlit night. Wolf is Dog's reclusive cousin, who kept to his wild ways after Dog aligned himself with humankind; not for Wolf a warm hearth and table scraps. Instead, Wolf remained in the wilderness. Only the wild places are reflected in the keen, honest mirrors of Wolf's eyes. Perhaps this is why our modern mainstream culture is wary and unsure of Wolf, typecasting him in myths and fables from Little Red Riding Hood to the Werewolf as a villain. But when those of us who revere the wild things look into those clear eyes, we see the soul of a being much more able than ourselves to accept the totality of life, the hard but necessary cycles — birth and death, feast and famine, gain and loss — of which all life is made. And when the sun is just right, or the moon is full, we may catch a glimpse in those eyes of our own frightened faces and realize how little we know of the world's grit. Wolf has much to teach us if we have the courage to learn.

Wolf hunts in packs and because of this can bring down deer, moose and caribou which can be as much as ten times Wolf's own weight. Wolf usually kills only the young, the old, the weak and the sick. In this manner, Wolf helps to keep a species strong by preventing the weak and the sick from multiplying. Call upon Wolf to help you eliminate your own weakness and non-productive thoughts. For those who put themselves down and are too hard on themselves, pray to Wolf to show you how to eliminate thoughts and feelings that weaken the spirit.

Wolf packs must hunt in a large territory in order to insure an adequate food supply. Howling helps Wolf to proclaim, define and defend his territory. Wolf medicine is about speaking up for and defining that which is rightfully ours. And since Wolf travels over long distances within his vast territory, Wolf medicine helps those who seek to journey far physically, mentally and spiritually.

Besides defending his territory, another reason Wolf howls is so that other Wolves will be aware of his pack's location. It is important that rival wolf packs give each other as much room as possible to reduce the chances of confrontation, because when such sharp fangs and fighting hearts meet there can be serious injury. This is avoided by scent marking and howling. Wolf shows us that those who are the most powerful do not need to prove their power and strength, but in fact make an effort to minimize conflict and diffuse tense situations.

Wolf mates for life and is the essence of loyal attachment. If you long for one kindred spirit to go through life with, pray to Wolf for assistance in finding, cherishing and keeping your mate. Wolf is also very loyal to his family. Those who seek to bond or heal a family relationship can pray to Wolf for this as well.

Wolves walk single file as they set off to search for prey, and at the head of the line walks the smartest, strongest wolf — the Medicine Wolf of the pack. Call upon Medicine Wolf if you want to develop leadership abilities. He teaches us that there are great responsibilities to leadership and great challenges as well, but if you have a unique and worthy vision to bring to the world, he will help you walk ahead of the rest and lead others to a higher path. Medicine Wolf also has great medicine power as a guide or teacher, especially in areas that are new, vanguard or on the cutting edge. Invoke Wolf for innovative, creative wisdom and the courage to act on it.

Wolf Invocation

May my spirit range far and wide.
May my heart endure and abide.
Grant me courage and loyalty.
Wolf Spirits, live in me!

Diane Versteeg

*is an artist whose love for animals
is beautifully expressed by the
drawings in this book. She specializes exclusively in animal art, and
is available for commissions on a
freelance basis. Limited edition
prints and posters are also available from the artist. She may be
contacted at PO box # 4048,
Palm Desert, CA 92260.*

Books by Dolfyn

CRYSTAL WISDOM:
Spiritual Properties of Crystals and Gemstones

Beautifully written, this is a clear, comprehensive yet easy-to-read guide toward greater insight and deeper understanding of the spiritual values and potentials of crystals and gemstones. *Crystal Wisdom* stresses your natural ability to communicate directly with crystals and other spirit stones without the need to master complex systems. This joyous book is a loving and friendly guide to tapping your own crystal wisdom. (ISBN# 0-929268-14-8)

SHAMANIC WISDOM:
Nature Spirituality, Sacred Power and Earth Ecstasy

This profoundly beautiful book inspires the reader to apply shamanic wisdom to everyday life. Among topics covered: how to create a medicine wheel, find our sacred clan name, raise medicine power, retrieve our animal spirit guardian and much more. Emphasizes the reader's ability to communicate with the spirit realm and have a loving relationship with Earth Mother. (ISBN # 0-929268-16-4)

SHAMANIC WISDOM VOL. II:
The Way of the Animal Spirits

In this companion volume to the best seller *Shamanic Wisdom*, the authors give a detailed account of the medicine powers of over seventy animals which are deeply revered by various tribal peoples around the world. The reader learns how to invoke animal spirit powers into themselves. The authors also take the reader into the everyday lives of the animals, so that an intensely practical and shamanic awareness of the animal spirit realm is gained. (0-929268-18-0)

ANGELIC WISDOM:
Celestial Beings and Their Spiritual Powers

Finally, a concise, easy-to-read book listing over fifty angels with a detailed description of their divine powers. Only positive angels are included — no fallen angels in this book! The angels are arranged alphabetically for the reader's convenience. Included are angel prayers and meditations that attune us to the particular angel. Thoroughly researched and clearly written, this is THE definitive book on angels. (0-929268-19-9)

Booklets by Dolfyn

Bough Down: Praying with Tree Spirits Teaches the reader how to communicate directly with trees in order to benefit from their healing guidance and love.

Attracting Love: The Art of Enchantment with Spirit Help How to work with spirit and medicine power to attract the person just right for you.

Praying with Fire: Communicating with Fire Spirits Teaches how to communicate with Fire Spirits, whose warmth and passion are akin to ours.

Crystal Connection: Finding Your Soulmate Channeled through a quartz crystal. Covers how to find one's soulmate and discover fulfillmemt.

More Booklets by Dolfyn

Shamanism, Vol. 1: A Beginner's Guide How to create a medicine wheel, go on a vision quest, meet our spiritual guardians, find our animal clan name and more.

Shamanism, Vol. 2: Working with Moon Medicine Increase your own medicine power by acting in harmony with the phases of the moon.

Shamansim, Vol. 3: Animal Medicine Powers Over 80 animals, their corresponding medicine powers and how to invoke and invite those powers into yourself.

Shamanism and Nature Spirituality: The Sacred Circle Covers step-by-step guidance necessary to create your own medicine wheel or sacred circle.

New Age Reference Charts by Dolfyn

8 1/2" by 11" two-sided, laminated reference charts. Clearly written and concise, these charts pack a lot of information in a small space.

Angels Lists 60 angels & their specific spiritual powers.

Attracting Love The art of enchantment with spirit help.

Attracting Money The art of prosperity with spirit help.

Animal Medicine Powers This chart covers over 70 animals & their medicine powers.

Animal Spirit Guardians How to befriend, communicate with and retrieve your animal guardian.

Attune to the Moon All basic aspects of moon medicine, moon magic, moon mystery are covered in this chart.

Crystal Wisdom Lists the new age crystals and gemstones with a brief description of their spiritual properties.

The Way of the Tree Spirits Covers the medicine powers and transformational properties of over 60 trees.

Psychic Protection Covers all the basics.

Shamanic Wisdom: A beginner's guide.